A SAUNTER THROUGH KENT WITH PEN AND PENCIL.

BY CHARLES IGGLESDEN.

ILLUSTRATED BY X. Willis.

PUBLISHED AT THE OFFICES OF THE KENTISH EXPRESS ASHFORD KENT.

1901

CONTENTS.

ILLUSTRATIONS.

———

EASTWELL.

The Mansion (Part of the Front)—Plantagenet's Cottage—The Tower
The Church from the Lake—A Plantagenet.

ELHAM.

A Bracket on the "Smithies' Arms"—A Charity Scholar
Corbels in the Church—The Manor House
Old Mantelpiece at "Smithies' Arms."

LYMINGE.

Alms Box in Church—A Saxon Window—St. Ethelburga's Tomb
Cardinal Morton's Tower—St. Eadburgh's Well.

ALLINGTON.

The Latticed Gate—Fireplace in Inner Court—A Peep from the Garden
In the Dovecote—The Entrance Gateway—At the Lock.

AYLESFORD.

The Bridge and Church—The Chequers—Kit's Coty House
The Countless Stones—A Double Dormer—The Old George.

CARMELITE PRIORY.

In the Courtyard—The Friars from the Garden—The Entrance Gate
An Old Corner—A Medallion with a Weird History.

PREFACE TO THE THIRD VOLUME.

The generous welcome accorded the first and second Volumes of this Work has induced me to issue a third. It will be noticed that in this Volume the articles are of somewhat greater length than in the earlier ones, for the deeper one dives into the historic associations and relics of Kent the richer and more abundant they become.

CHARLES IGGLESDEN.

Ashford,
    December 2nd, 1901.

PRINTED AT THE KENTISH EXPRESS OFFICE,
94, HIGH STREET, ASHFORD.

A Saunter Through Kent

With Pen and Pencil.

By CHARLES IGGLESDEN.

A Phenomenal Success has attended the publication of this work. There are many Sketches of the picturesque towns, villages and hamlets of the county, old houses and historic spots. Local traditions and legends are a feature of the work.

Price 2/6 per Volume.

The Complete Work of Ten Volumes can be had for £1 1/- Post Free

Published at the Kentish Express Office, Ashford.

EASTWELL HOUSE PART OF THE FRONT

PLANTAGANETS COTTAGE

THE TOWER

THE CHURCH FROM THE LAKE:

EASTWELL.

———

ONE of the most sparsely populated villages in Kent, owning not a public-house and not even the ubiquitous lollipop shop, yet brimful of strange traditions and historical associations such as many a town fifty times its size would give untold gold to possess. Such is Eastwell, lying to the north-west of Ashford, along the Faversham road, the walls of its timber-laden park flanking the highway on the left-hand side.

The "royal village" some call Eastwell, and for two appropriate reasons. In the first place one of the Plantagenets lived and died here in the person of the natural son of King Richard the Third; in the second place the late Duke of Saxe Coburg-Gotha, then Duke of Edinburgh, resided here for eleven years, and Eastwell House was the birth-place of his two daughters—Princess Marie and Princess Beatrice.

But there are many other remarkable things to be recorded about the village—fact and fiction; in the latter category being quite a pretty collection of ghost stories to shudder over while sauntering under the trees of the park which occupies nearly all the acres of the parish.

Yes, it is a tiny dot in the county but it will take some considerable time to write its history. There are so many unique features about Eastwell. For instance, it extends on one side as far as Sandyhurst, where, curious to say, the boundaries of East-well, Westwell, Boughton Aluph, Kennington and Ashford meet within a space of 20 perches. Mr. Foster when at Sandyhurst Farm used to amuse his friends by pointing out to them that he lived in Ashford; that his men had to go to Kennington to attend to the horses; that the dairymaids went to Eastwell to milk cows; while his waggon lodge was also in the latter parish. Lenacre Street is partly in Eastwell and partly in Boughton Aluph; unfortunately, owing to modern vandalism, the parish boundary stone which stood in the hedgerow close to where two yew trees can now be seen was broken and destroyed. In the opposite direction the bounds of the parish extend to the fringe of Boughton Green.

Eastwell is a parish of wells : hence its designation. It possesses at least three notable wells, but the one from which it derives its name is that at the end of the wood westward of the church. This well, which at the present time supplies water to the House, was undoubtedly in earlier days a sacred spring and was dedicated to the Virgin Mary—"Our Lady"—the favourite patron saint of the district. At the present day it is known as the "Lady Well," and undoubtedly the original name of the parish was "East of the Well," as Westwell was in all probability called "West of the Well."

Plantagenet's Well lies within a stone's throw of Plantagenet's Cottage, near the gas works on the Boughton road. It is between twenty and thirty feet deep and for a long time was the receptacle for all kinds of rubbish. It was an object of interest until about six years ago when it was filled up with building refuse and thereby closed. A railing now cuts off that part of the park, but two fine trees standing close together mark the historic spot. Locally the cottage is credited as having been the home of Richard Plantagenet, and with being the very house he built when he was permitted by Sir Thomas Moyle, the builder of Eastwell House, to end his days at Eastwell. But more of the remarkable history of the Royal bricklayer anon.

The "Countess's Well" is close to the upper end of the lake and is supposed to be very ancient. Close by at one time ran a road, and it is surmised that in the vicinity a former Eastwell House stood, and that this well provided the water supply. In it have been found some curious bricks and a beaten leaden pipe.

Eastwell lies right on the Pilgrims' Way, and it may be interesting to state that it continues to be visited by modern pilgrims from many parts of the earth. The old Pilgrims' Road through the Park, which is now unfortunately a thing of the past, used to run by the Church and left the Park by the side of the Gas House, close to Boughton Green. In fact the old footpath through the

Park which ran from Eastwell Church, past the Reading Room, and out on to the Faversham Road, was the actual way used by the Pilgrims themselves, but this path was diverted a few years ago by Lord Gerard when the extensive alterations at the House were carried out.

Like many another village, Eastwell has changed in appearance to a great extent during the past 60 or 70 years. Years ago there was an old thoroughfare known as the Old Charing Lane, which was used principally by Westwell people as a " short cut " to the Faversham Road. It branched at Tumbledown from the present lane leading from Westwell Church to Lenacre Street, and passing close to the Church at Eastwell emerged from the Park into the Faversham Road close by the new vicarage. The old Earl of Winchilsea desired to have this road stopped and he took the necessary steps to have his desires gratified. But the people of Westwell were incensed at the thought of being deprived of their rights, and they opposed the application when it came before the Courts. They were successful, but it cost the parish something like £200. A second application on behalf of the Earl was unopposed on account of the heavy law costs incurred on the previous occasion and the road was therefore closed. The bad feeling caused thereby continued to exist for a long time, and one farmer, more independent than the rest, planted a hop-garden on land of his own, which bordered the Park, and could be seen from Eastwell House. The Earl was so annoyed at this that he had a belt of trees planted round the garden, but it was some time before they became large enough to hide the plantation from the House.

Having dwelt upon the leading points of Eastwell's history, let us take our saunter through it. We come by way of Kennington, and find, confronting us, the imposing entrance tower, bright and glittering in its dressing of flint and Caen stone. It may be safely classed as unique in its structure as the flints used in the facing were all carefully cut into squares, a difficult task as one may imagine, and to accomplish this it cost the owner $2\frac{1}{2}$d. for each flint to be worked to a smooth surface. Its erection, however, was not accomplished without mishap, for one of the workmen, making a mis-step, fell from a high scaffolding and was killed on the spot. An extensive and enchanting view of the valley between Eastwell and the sea at Folkestone and Hythe is obtainable from the top of the Tower, with the lofty tower of Ashford church and the fertile pastures of the Weald of Kent. In the inner apartment of the tower is a large picture in Italian tile work, erected when the place was built in 1843. The subject is Alexander gaining one of his brilliant victories. The tower actually stands in Boughton parish.

Leaving the tower on our right we stroll along Lenacre Street. At one time it was graced by a fine old residence known as Lenacre Hall, which stood on the left-hand side of the road going towards Westwell in the field facing the end of the Park wall. But the house stood in the wrong parish, as the old Earl, whose one desire was to have Eastwell as select a place possible, with no houses beyond those absolutely necessary for the needs of the estate, had it pulled down. Many of the bricks were thrown into the cellar and the site on which the house stood can now be identified by a hollow in the field caused through the debris in the cellar subsiding. The present Lenacre Farm, which is in Boughton parish, was in those days attached to Lenacre Hall as a waggoner's house, but it was enlarged on the old hall being demolished.

Opposite, on our right, can be seen the termination of the wall which edges the Park from Rattle Hall, at Challock, to Lenacre Street, a distance of over four miles. This great wall, it is interesting to learn, was built throughout by a Boughton man named Austen and his sons, and the bricks used in its construction were all made on the estate. The wall was erected in two stages. The first portion ended at a spot midway between the new vicarage at Boughton and the stream which passes under the road—which, by the way, ran over the highway before the road was diverted and the hill leading to the tower lowered. At that time duty had to be paid on each thousand of bricks, and consequently they were made as large as possible. But during the three or four years which elapsed before the work was resumed the brick tax was removed, and a smaller and neater brick was consequently made. By a close examination of the wall at the spot indicated one can easily see where the work was discontinued and resumed again by the difference in the size of the bricks used.

Resuming our stroll up Lenacre Street we notice the quaint cottages which stand at the end of the wall. The peculiar windows strike the eye and it is a curious fact that similar windows can be seen in all the old cottages on the estate. This peculiarity is even noticeable in the labourers' tenements adjoining the oasthouses at Bybrook Farm, close to the Ashford and Kennington boundary on the Canterbury Road, a holding which was formerly included in the Eastwell Estate.

It was in the first of these cottages in Lenacre Street that one of the most peculiar characters of Eastwell lived. Known as "Old Mother Hubbard," she was a most eccentric person, and an extraordinary tale is told respecting her husband's death. The honest old fellow got so weak in his last hours that he could not take pills he had been supplied with, and his wife innocently confided to her neighbours after his death that she managed to make John take his pills for she stood behind his bed and every time he opened his mouth—whilst gasping for breath—she popped one in! But the poor old soul, who, by the way ended her days in Willesborough Workhouse, loved her husband dearly. After his death she would always place his plate and knife and fork in their accustomed place on the dinner table, and would remark that she was "never tired of waiting on John." She actually took the trouble to carry John's watch, after his death, to a neighbour's house at Goat Lees each night to have it wound up! Among other eccentricities she collected old clothes, and when her effects were sold they contained a hundred dresses, and a similar number of detached pockets which ladies, in bygone days, used to dangle from their waists. She also kept a remarkable herd of pigs, to each of which she gave a name.

Continuing along the road we come to the field adjoining the two houses on the left-hand side of the road, in which the parish almshouse used to stand. The house was intended for the inhabitant of the parish possessing the largest family, he or she having the privilege of living there rent free. This house eventually met the same fate as the old Lenacre Hall and its last occupant was a man named Moon, an old estate servant. The terms of the charity must have been either overlooked or evaded in this case for Moon had only one child. He was a quaint character, and an odd tale is told respecting him. He was a little thin man and had the misfortune to possess an exceedingly fat wife. To the old Earl, who was on intimate terms with the whole of his workmen, Moon was wont to bemoan what would be his fate when old age overtook him and when he would be unable to work. At last the Earl good-naturedly told Moon that he should never want so long as he (the Earl) lived, and he installed him in the almshouse directly it became empty. He was supplied with the servants' cast-off livery, and also with food from the Earl's kitchen. The latter he used to take home, but, probably owing to his thin wizened appearance and the corresponding plumpness of his better half, gossips stated that Mrs. Moon robbed her husband of his food and half starved him. This got to the ears of the Earl, who, on meeting Moon, said, "Hang me!"—a favourite expression of his—"You shall have your food at the House where I can see you eat it!" And his lordship was as good as his word, for from that day until he lay on his death-bed Moon was served with the same choice viands which the family partook of and these he ate from the Earl's dining-room window-sill.

A lovely stroll round the bend, which, by the way, possesses the quaint title of "Rump Corner," and is named as such on the tithe map of the parish, past the old Rectory, which has now been converted into a shooting box by Mr. Holden, through the narrow winding lane brings us to a sharp turning on the right leading to the lake and the church.

Here we find one of the most beautiful views in Kent—a miniature Windermere. The old bridge; the ivy-mantled church; the sombre yews backed by the tall trees of the churchyard and, further away, by the wooded downs; the old buttressed cottage almost hidden in the foliage and its garden running down to the water's-edge; the glassy surface of the islet-dotted lake. Yes, it forms a picture of beauty to which the brush of the truest artist could scarce do justice. The bridge upon which we stand and spans the stream that feeds the lake was erected in 1845, principally from surplus material when the tower was completed.

The church is of Perpendicular architecture. The interior is rich in carving and a striking peculiarity may be observed in the beautifully carved chancel screen and the pew poppy-heads. Every panel in the former is delicately worked to a design different from the others, while none of the numerous poppy-heads are alike. Many bear saintly figures, while others have carved heads, acorns, griffins, dragons and other figures, while one in the south aisle has an open book with the sacred initials "I.H.S." inscribed on the open pages. The head of the pew in the south aisle which was used by members of the Finch-Hatton family has a rebus carved upon it. The figure of a small bird represents "Finch," and the family name is completed by a hat and a tun (a cask) beneath, thus making Finch-Hatton.

When it was customary for the sexes to be separated at Divine service the Earl of Winchilsea occupied a pew in the middle aisle, the one which was used by the Duke of Edinburgh and his children, and now by the present occupiers of Eastwell House, and the poppy-head here bears the image of St. Peter with the keys. Lady Winchilsea had a seat opposite, in the north aisle, and here the representation is that of a woman, probably that of the Virgin Mary.

The sacred edifice is likewise rich in monuments, the most beautiful of which is in the south aisle, erected by George William, Earl of Winchilsea, to the memory of his second wife Emily Georgiana, who died on July 10th, 1858, at the early age of 39 years. Her ladyship, who was one of the most beautiful women of the day and at one time a great favourite at Court, was niece of the Duke of Wellington and maid of honour to Queen Adelaide, and she gave to the church the costly communion plate which is at present in use. The four verses which are inscribed on the sides of the monument were composed by herself and were found under her pillow after her death. The monument bears a figure, said to be an exact likeness of the Countess, reclining on a couch with a scroll held by her right hand, bearing the words, " I am happy indeed, happy in the Word, God is waiting for me." The verses, which have a touch of pathos in them and to which are appended the composer's initials, E.G.W. and N. (Emily Georgiana Winchilsea and Nottingham), are as follows :—

When the knell rung for the dying
  Soundeth for me ;
And my corse coldly is lying
  'Neath the green tree.

When the turf strangers are heaping
  Covers my breast,
Come not to gaze on the weeping,
  I am at rest.

All my life coldly and sadly,
  The days have gone by ;
I, who dreamed wildly and madly,
  Am happy to die.

Long since my heart has been breaking,
  Its pain is past,
A time has been set to its aching,
  Peace comes at last.

The vein of sadness which runs through this burial poem can better be understood by those cognisant of the composer's unfortunate history, and of the terrible misfortune—kleptomania—over which she had no control, which blighted her young life, and no doubt broke her heart. The monument is the work of one of the best known sculptors of Rome and was finished in 1850.

In the south chancel is another magnificent tomb with recumbent life-size figures erected to the memory of Sir Moyle Finch, who is clad in armour and was one of Queen Elizabeth's Privy Councillors, and his widow, the first Countess of Winchilsea and Nottingham, honours conferred on her in recognition of her husband's services to the State. Formerly this tomb was enriched by a dome or canopy supported by eight pillars of black marble, but this disappeared long before the recollection of any living person. It is said that the canopy was taken down by one of the old Earls of Winchilsea.

Close by is another large tomb to members of the Moyle family (the first one of whom, Sir Thomas Moyle, re-built Eastwell House and died in 1560). Curiously enough the vault beneath the tomb has recently been found to be completely empty, there being not the slightest trace of a coffin or of any other signs of the interment of bodies therein. A short time ago a portion of the vault fell in, and it was then that it was explored and found to be empty.

Hung above on the walls of the church can be seen three of the helmets which belonged to the Finch family.

Against the north wall, within the communion rails, is an ancient monument of Bethersden marble, which, tradition says, denotes the burial place of Sir Richard Plantagenet. The fact that the tomb originally had two brasses and a supplicatory prayer such as "Jesu, Mercy," or "Mary, Help," repeated four times on scrolls at the corners, leads archæologists of the present day to confidently declare that the tomb is not that of Plantagenet, while additional doubt is cast on the tradition by the surmise that Sir Thomas Moyle, who held high State offices, including that of Speaker in the House of Commons, would not risk incurring Royal displeasure by erecting such a monument to the son of a king whose identity he had helped to hide. Further than that, in 1720 Dr. Brett, of Spring Grove, Wye, a very learned divine of his day, who resigned the Rectories of Betteshanger and Ruckinge because his conscience would not permit him to take the oaths then imposed by the Government, distinctly stated in a letter that beyond the entry in the register there was no other "memorial" of Plantagenet, and it could not be said whether he was buried in the church or in the churchyard.

Beneath the church floor, at the upper end of the south aisle, and covered with a large slab in which are affixed a couple of rings, is the immense vault in which were placed the remains of many members of the Finch family. Mr. Edward Hatton, uncle of George William, Earl of Winchilsea, was the last one buried in the vault, which was closed for interments when the church was restored and reseated in 1842, owing to the subterraneous chamber being partly filled with water. The coffins it contained, which were of lead, and many of which were of curious shape, were placed on ledges by the sides of the vault, and in 1771 when the Hon. Edward Finch-Hatton was buried there Hasted in his History of Kent states that there were 38 coffins in the vault.

The sacred edifice contains in the west a very rich stained-glass window. The remarkable part of its history is that it was constructed from a collection of ancient glass, gathered from many places of note by the father of the late Earl of Winchilsea. The fragments include Royal coats of Arms, including two of Queen Elizabeth's, one dated 1570. Another fact which makes the window remarkable is that the person who placed the pieces of glass in position turned portions upside down, thus making it heraldically wrong.

Originally the square embattled tower contained three bells, but many persons can recollect when it had but one. This fact gained it the same curious ditty that Charing church possessed when it had only a solitary bell:—

> "Eastwell Church lies in a hole;
> It has but one bell and that was stole."

This was no doubt as much a slander on Eastwell as it was in the case of Charing, for although there is no trace of the fate of the other two original bells, there is no doubt that the one still hanging in the tower was one of the peal. It bears the inscription, "T. Mears, fecit, tenor, 1794." The remaining five bells were given by the Earl of Winchilsea in 1842, when the sacred edifice was restored.

Right in the corner of the south chancel is a curious little square gallery where the old barrel organ, which for many years led the singing, was played. The font, which is of stone, is richly carved in keeping with the other parts of the church, and the beautifully carved oak lectern, together with the lamps, was given by Mr.

H. A. Campbell, a former resident at the House, while the harmonium, which is still in use, was presented by the late Duke of Edinburgh.

It will probably surprise many to learn that the site of the church is much higher than those at Ashford, Kennington or Wye. It stands on ground 238 feet above sea level, whereas Ashford is only 187 feet, Wye but 157 and Kennington 201. On the other hand the site of Boughton Aluph church, which stands on a hill, is 267 feet above sea level.

The principal characteristic of the churchyard is its neat and tidy appearance. It contains the graves of three members of the Winchilsea family and a peculiar feature, unnoticed by many who visit the spot, is the inscription cut on the face of the rugged stones which surround the graves. It runs thus :—" Thousands of toiling hands where theirs have ceased from their labour ; thousands of weary feet where theirs have completed their journey ; thousands of throbbing hearts where theirs are at rest and for ever ; thousands of aching brains where theirs no longer are busy."

There is an interesting history attached to the neat slabs of slate placed over numerous graves in the churchyard. Formerly the familiar mounds denoted where there were graves, but these were displeasing to the eye of the old Earl, who desired that the turf should be kept cut short. Accordingly, when he was chosen as churchwarden during the ministry of the late Rev. M. Oxenden, he suggested that the mounds should be levelled and slate slabs laid down so that a mowing machine could be used to cut the grass. The vicar objected, pointing out to the Earl that such an action would put the parish to a great expense, but my lord replied, " I am the parson's master, and I will do what I like." And he did. The graves were levelled, the slate slabs laid down, the cost falling upon the parish, and from that day to this Eastwell churchyard has proved to be one of the best kept within a radius of a good many miles. The sequel was that the Earl was never again elected churchwarden.

But the Earl was sincere in his religion, a fact which can be gathered from the following interesting anecdote. The old turnpike gate at Goat Lees was kept at one time by a man named Fullager, and on one occasion the Earl got into conversation with the old fe'low, from whom he learned the fact that his duties prevented him from attending church on the Sabbath. " Hang me !" replied the noble visitor, "I will keep the gate for you next Sunday so that you can go to church." And he did, but probably profiting by his monotonous duties and his peculiar experience he never repeated the experiment.

An ancient yew tree at one time stood in the churchyard, but it disappeared in 1828, being blown down and entirely destroyed during a memorable gale in that year.

Before concluding the history of the church and its surroundings, I might mention that in 1822 the chancel was paved with large square tiles, laid on bricks, to prevent dampness, and five years later the roof of the chancel was removed and a new one constructed at a cost of £389. The living of the adjoining parish of Boughton Aluph was united with that of Eastwell in 1894, during the incumbency of the Rev. Martin Reed.

The old cottage which lies beyond the church is undoubtedly the oldest building in the parish. It possesses flint walls of extraordinary thickness, and there are immense buttresses to strengthen the walls between five and six feet in depth of more modern date. All the floors are of thick oak, and in the passages can be seen partitions made from the large old fashioned pew doors, which were taken from the church when it was reseated between fifty and sixty years ago. The house was originally built for the occupier of the farm which, prior to the construction of the lake, existed partly on its site. And a fertile holding it must have been if one can judge from the glowing accounts which are still given by old inhabitants of the immense crops of hops that grew in the valley now covered by the waters of the lake. "Ah," said one old picker, "dey were hops, an' no mistake. You couldn't see de alleys for hops and dere was always hops no matter what de season." And the age of the plantation was never known, the only guide being one of the poles, which was of yew and which bore a date at the last picking over a century back. This particular pole was treasured as a relic by the occupier of the farm, who had it safely housed every time it was pulled. But it disappeared many years ago.

The lake, one of the most beautiful in the south of England, covers an area of nearly forty acres, and prior to its construction about sixty years ago a small stream ran down the valley in the centre. Soon after the lake was made a miniature man-of-war could be seen sailing on its waters. It belonged to the old Earl of Winchilsea, was rigged with sails and fitted with dummy Jack Tars and guns made of wood. The skipper was a well-known local character named Jack Creed, who had been a soldier in his time. But one night, during a gale, the craft came to grief. It was blown ashore near the church, and became a total wreck, her timbers remaining on the mud bank for years before they rotted away. When the lake was emptied and cleaned out a few years ago a small iron rowing boat was discovered embedded in the mud. This was built to satisfy the boyish fad of one of the younger members of the family, but it had not long been in use when it sank, its occupant almost losing his life. This relic can now be seen at the rear of the old cottage at the back of the church.

Leaving the churchyard by a path leading in the direction of the House, we come within sight of Plantagenet Cottage. And this recalls to mind the strange story of Richard Plantagenet. There is no doubt but that this royal person was, during the erection of the old Eastwell House by Sir Thomas Moyle, engaged as chief brick-layer, and whenever he left off work he retired to some corner with a book. It was this strange behaviour that first aroused the curiosity of Sir Thomas, who watched the scholar and finally surprised him with a Latin book in his hand. To be able to read Latin in those days was a privilege enjoyed only by those in high position of life. Upon being closely questioned the royal bricklayer confided in Sir Thomas the secret he had never before revealed to anyone. The following is the family tradition told by Heneage, Earl of Winchilsea, to Dr. Brett in the autumn of 1720 :—Plantagenet was boarded with a Latin schoolmaster, without knowing who his parents were until he was 15 or 16 years old. A gentleman, who told him that he was no relation to him, visited him once a quarter, paid his board, and saw that he wanted for nothing. One eventful day this person took him from school to a fine great house and left him alone in one of the stately rooms. Then a man, finely dressed, wearing star and garter, came to him, questioned him and gave him some money. Plantagenet was then taken back to school, but a short time after-wards his quarterly visitor arrived with a spare horse and told him that he must prepare to take a journey into the country. They went into Leicestershire, came to Bosworth Field, and the lad was carried to King Richard the Third's tent. The King embraced him, and after telling him that he was his son, said, " But, child, to-morrow I must fight for my Crown. And assure yourself, if I lose, that I will lose my life too. But I hope to preserve both." The

King directed him to stand at a certain spot where he could witness the coming battle with safety, and then continued, "And when I have gained the victory come to me; I will then own you to be mine and take care of you. But if I should be so unfortunate as to lose the battle, then shift as well as you can, and take care to let nobody know that I am your father, for no mercy will be shown to anyone so nearly related to me." After receiving a purse of gold from the King's hands, Plantagenet went to the spot indicated by his father, and witnessed the battle in which the King was slain. He then proceeded to London, where he disposed of his horse and "fine cloths" and apprenticed himself to the calling of a bricklayer. He spent all his spare time in educating himself in secret, and eventually came to Eastwell, where, as stated above, he acted as chief bricklayer during the erection of the old Eastwell House. On discovering Plantagenet's identity Sir Thomas Moyle said to him, "You are now old and almost past your labour; I will give you the run of my kitchen as long as you live." Plantagenet declined this offer, saying, "Sir, you have a numerous family; I have been used to live retired; give me leave to build a house of one room for myself in such a field, and there, with your good leave, I will live and die." This humble request Sir Thomas complied with, Plantagenet built his house, and lived in it until his death.

Dr. Brett computed that Plantagenet was about 81 years old when he died, and stated that the father of Lord Heneage pulled down the house, which, after its erection, was enclosed in the park, and his lordship, in telling him of the demolition of the building, remarked, "I would as soon have pulled down Eastwell House." This would seem to entirely dispose of the local traditions that either the building now known as Plantagenet Cottage or the curious little erection in the park termed "Little Jack's House" was the dwelling which Plantagenet erected and lived in. The former is no doubt very ancient, for its walls, which are of burnt earth and ballast, are about eighteen inches thick. The windows are of the shape peculiar to all the cottages on the estate, and the front door inside the massive porch is of oak, between two and three inches thick, coffer-panelled and studded with large-headed nails. The porch is very remarkable, being built of solid brickwork and carried up high above the roof. In the summer time it is covered with Virginia creeper, but with the falling leaf a dummy window is visible. There is an almost square cellar beneath one of the rooms, and this is credited with having been the hiding place of Plantagenet in times of necessity.

The village school, which provides accommodation for the children of both Eastwell and Boughton Aluph, and which stands just within the boundary of the former parish, is a peculiarly constructed building; and one of the tie beams in the large room at once strikes the attention of the visitor as being exactly like those at Wye College. Formerly a girls' school existed at the back of the present buildings, but this was demolished half-a century ago.

The park, which comprises about 2,000 acres, is thickly wooded, with an undulating surface: in fact, the Kentish Downs run through it. In four parishes—Westwell, Challock, Boughton Aluph and East-well—stands the park, but the Eastwell estate extends to much wider limits. Although now well wooded the tree feller's axe has within the last decade or two robbed the park of much of its beauty. The old Earl took a great pride in the timber on his estate, and soon after his death, when the Duke of Edinburgh desired to make Eastwell a permanent Royal residence, the wood alone was valued at £250,000. One noble oak stood on the forty-acre plain and was known as "Straight Oak," and rose to a height of between forty and fifty feet. An offer of £50 for it was refused by the Earl, but at length the giant fell to decay. Another oak close by was of almost similar dimensions, and it may be of interest to know that out of one length alone sixteen swing gates were made. A third oak was specially felled in order to find timber for the construction of the hall table at Eastwell House.

Many of the beautiful walks through the park have with the change of owners and tenants been stopped, but there are still several lovely strolls open to the public. One of the most picturesque is that leading from Eastwell church to Challock church, past the front of the House; another, branching off to the left of Eastwell church, leads to Westwell, emerging into the hilly lane from West-well water mill to Challock Lees, known as Dunn Street: and a third in the opposite direction runs past the lake into the Faver-sham road, emerging either at the first gatehouse past the Tower or at Eastwell schools.

Speaking of the paths in the park reminds me of an amusing story of the old Earl. During one of his strolls in the park he saw a sweep take a short cut. He went forward to stop him, but the knight of the chimney was obstinate and refused to go back. A rough and tumble ensued, and although the Earl proved the victor he emerged from the fray quite as black as his opponent, who, by·

the-bye, was quite unconscious of his victor's identity. It was one of the jokes that the old Earl told at his own expense.

The path from the church to Challock church is highly interesting and picturesque. Leaving the church and lake behind we take a path in the direction of the house. Soon we come to the forty-acre plain, the fine piece of open ground facing the house. It was on this spot that the Earl of Winchilsea was wont to practice previous to his famous duel with the Duke of Wellington. The two noblemen had quarrelled in the "Parliament House," and determined to restore their honour by the prevailing custom of fighting a duel at Eastwell. The owner of Eastwell was a dead shot, but he was not idle during the short interval which elapsed between the challenge and the fight. Almost daily would he stroll into the park, fix up a target, step out the requisite number of paces which were to separate him and the Duke on the duel day, and fire over his shoulder. And despite the fact that he was firing with his back to the target he would hit it nine times out of ten. Old residents at Eastwell hand down stories which their parents have told them of the Earl's deadly aim, and one person relates that one day whilst his mother was out in the park thistle cutting the Earl came along, took the spud out of her hands, thrust it in the ground, and firing at it with his back turned shattered the handle with the bullet. Fortunately, through the Earl's magnanimity, the duel, which was fought in Battersea Fields, London, on March 21st, 1829, had a happy ending. The Duke had the first shot, and, being deadly in earnest, fired as point-blank as was possible with his back turned at his adversary. The bullet, however, missed the Earl, who, instead of retaliating, simply fired into the air to show that he bore no animosity to the Duke. Thus the quarrel ended and honour was restored on both sides. But the Duke admired the Earl's generous action, and subsequently presented him, as a memento of the event, with a costly inlaid pianoforte.

But to return to the forty-acre plain. Just to the left is the reservoir and near here used to stand "Little Jack's house." It was a brick building of two rooms, one on top of the other. Each contained a fireplace, but nothing is known for what purpose it was used beyond the statement that it was utilised for the isolation of a horse suffering from glanders. Until it became too ruinous for use buck beans were stored in it. There is a local tradition that the Plantagenet outcast hid there, but no conclusive evidence can be gleaned.

We now take another path; now, alas! no longer a thoroughfare. It leads from the church straight to a plain grass-covered mound— the mound that can be seen from Ashford and the whole of the valley below. This is Mount Pleasant, and as we near its summit we note solitary yews dotting its border—ragged old trees rugged with age. From this spot what a glorious panoramic view spreads itself before us! So high are we that the miles and miles below seem absolutely level, although, as a matter of fact, the country is undulating. On our left are the Wye Downs, with the village from which they derive their name nestling at their feet. Further south is the coast line, and on a clear day we can almost follow it till it reaches Fairlight, above Hastings, and the sails of passing craft and the smoke from steamers' funnels can be distinguished. Nearer, and below us, is the wooded park, the rich green of the pastures and the sombre tints of oak, beech and yew relieved by the glassy lake, its waters glittering in the sunlight. Farther away is Ashford, looking no bigger than a village in the distance. Then, as we cast our eye around in a more westerly direction there is the distant Weald of Kent, and, nearer to us, the wooded parks of Godinton, Hothfield and Surrenden, culminating in the chalk-clad summit of Westwell Downs, upon which beacons blazed in years gone by.

Leaving Mount Pleasant on the left, we follow a twisting path known as Winding Hill and come to one of the most delightful spots in Kent. It is known as the Star Walk, because here years ago there was a big clearing and from the open space ran beautiful avenues in the form of a star. In Hasted's time there were eight, and even forty years ago the starlike avenues could be easily distinguished. But the woodman's axe has upset the symmetry, while lightning and wind have played havoc with other monarchs of the forest, and now it is impossible to follow anything like the eight clear avenues. But some remain. One takes us to Challock Lees —the spot locally known as Brown's, while another brings us out on Challock Hill—the avenue which was once the main entrance to the park and house. The beech trees here are magnificent. Under their branches grow luxuriant bracken through which peer the round brown eyes of startled deer, and at our feet the soft turf sinks at every step. On a summer's day all is delightfully calm and shady, and the late Duke of Edinburgh was wont to entertain his guests to afternoon tea under the branches of the beeches. At night-time how changed is the scene. Owls screech overhead, strange insects rustle in the fallen leaves, shadows from overhanging branches flit across the path, and quaint trunks of lightning-stricken trees stand out from the gloom, white and barkiess, taking the shape of gigantic mortals or untameable beasts of the forest glade. No wonder that Eastwell is rich in ghost stories! a sensitive brain could conjure up many a weird-like fancy along the Star Walk at midnight.

Before railway communication came into vogue, when journeys had to be made to and from London by coach, the main entrance to Eastwell Park was through the noble avenue of elms near Challock church, and whenever the Eastwell coach arrived at night-time the drive through the avenue was illuminated by lanterns held aloft by boys.

The present house is modern, having been built by Colonel Finch-Hatton at a cost of about £50,000, a sum which, he used to boast, he saved whilst the work was being done. A new wing was added by the old Earl from a sum of half a million sterling left by Mr. Edward Hatton, better known to old inhabitants as "Teddy Hatton," to be spent on improving the estate, where he had spent many years of his life with his nephew. With this sum the lake was constructed and the bridge and entrance tower built. The extensive alterations and improvements recently carried out at a cost of half a million by Lord Gerard, who purchased the estate from the late Earl of Winchilsea, are within the recollection of my readers. Domesday mentions that in 1081 the place, then spelt Estwelle, belonged to Hugo de Montford, having been given to him in recognition of his services to the Conquerer with whom he fought at the Battle of Hastings. After a lapse to the Crown the estate descended to a family who took their surname from the name of the parish, then to the Criol family and on to Thomas de Poynings, the Earl of Northumberland, Sir Christopher Hales, Henry the Eighth's Attorney-General, Sir Thomas Moyle, Speaker of the House of Commons (who rebuilt the house in the sixteenth century), and to Sir Thomas Finch, whose eldest son, Sir Moyle Finch, embattled the old house, which he greatly enlarged, and enclosed a 1,000 acres for the park, Sir Moyle's widow was the first Vicountess Maidstone and Countess of Winchilsea. One of the descendants of the Finch family, Heneage, the second Earl of Winchilsea, had four wives, by whom he had twenty-seven children. The titles of Earl of Winchilsea and

Viscount Maidstone became extinct in 1728, but the second Earl of
Nottingham, son of Sir Heneage Finch, who succeeded to the estate, ultimately became the sixth Earl of Winchilsea. The double
title he possessed has been handed down to the present day, and the
estate remained in the possession of his descendants until its purchase
by Lord Gerard from the late Earl of Winchilsea. During the late
earl's ownership the tenants included Sir Albert Sassoon, the late
Duke of Edinburgh, the late Mr. H. A. Campbell, and Mr. H. V.
Holden. The late Lord Gerard resided there for a time, but upon
the present holder of the title coming into possession the house and
park were let to Mr. H. J. King.

The only manor included in Eastwell is that of Pothery, an
original possession of Odo, Bishop of Bayeaux, and which, with
that prelate's disgrace, was confiscated to the Crown and eventually
became included in the Eastwell Estate. The parish is likewise sadly
deficient in benefactions. One, however, deserves mention on account
of its curiosity. In 1480 Sir Walter Moyle, who accumulated a large
fortune as a lawyer, and who eventually rose to the dignity of
Speaker of the House of Commons, directed in his will that his
feoffees "shoald deliver an estate in fee simple to three or four
honest and trusty men, in two acres of arable land in this parish
called Cotingland, to the use of the Church of Eastwell, in recom-
pense of a certain annual rent of two pounds of wax, by him wrested
and detained from it against his conscience." The only other
charities were the almshouses which disappeared many years ago,
and a sixth part of an annual rent of £6, rental of a field at
Great Chart, left in 1680 by a Mr. Thomas Kipps. It is worthy
of note that the latter benefaction was divisible between six distinct
parishes.

Ghost stories connected with Eastwell Park are almost as
plentiful as blackberries. That which seems to be more commonly
related than the rest is one which depicts a coach drawn through the
park by four headless horses, with decapitated attendants sitting on
the box. You will still be told by old people that the rumbling
of the wheels on the turf has been heard, and that the apparition
suddenly disappears. Another ghost formerly "walked" the house and
grounds, but according to local tradition this was "laid" for a hundred
years, and will re-appear a few years hence.

Greater credence is, however, placed in the apparition seen in the
Park by two of the estate workmen a hundred years ago, and the

following account of it was told to the writer by a son of one of the men who actually witnessed it. The two men were coming home from work through the Park, and when about to pass through a clap-gate they noticed a man walking towards them. Although he passed over undulating ground his head remained on the same level. If he went up one of the hills only his head could be seen; if he went down through a valley still they saw his head, even though the hollow sank a hundred feet. Most mortals would have bolted, but these two stolidly remained at the gate to await the approach of this strange personage. As he came nearer one of the two stepped forward to open it, when, hey, presto! he disappeared, as if by magic, into space! My informant got the story from his father's lips.

On one occasion the wheels of the old Eastwell coach refused to run round owing, it is said, to some supernatural powers. The occupants had to alight and walk to the house, and it took a team of farm horses to remove the cumbrous vehicle. The more plausible explanation is that probably the wheels had locked through being " fired," but the simple country folk at once associated the occurrence with supernatural agencies. Anyhow, the coach was never used again, but torn to pieces and portions of it utilised for various purposes on the estate until a year or so ago.

Yet one more ghost story ere I finish. By more than one person in Ashford and Kennington I have heard it whispered that some forty years ago certain clergy of the neighbourhood met in the Park one midnight and under the flare of torches marched around the lake and with great solemnity "laid" the ghost. In the present days of enlightenment such action on the part of any clergyman seems impossible, and I for one cannot believe that such a superstitious proceeding would be tolerated in the Church of England. I, however, give the story for what it is worth. One explanation offered is that a meeting of clergy occurred at Eastwell, and after a ceremony in the church they walked in procession to the house. This may have given rise to the above story, and additional glamour was appended by the story-tellers transferring the time to midnight and introducing the torches.

The old parish register, the first entry in which is dated 1539, and which runs on to 1837, is an interesting document inasmuch as it contains the record of the burial at Eastwell of Richard Plantagenet on December 22nd, 1550, and of the interment of the majority of the members of the noble family who owned Eastwell for so long a period. The register shows that between 1664 and 1703—a space of 39 years—no less than seven ladies Finch were buried in the large vault at the upper end of the south aisle of the church. Sir Thomas Finch, one of the many owners of Eastwell of that name, we find was drowned "a little way from Rye Haylinge to Newhavenwards, March 19th, and buried March 23rd, 1564." Two further entries bear testimony to the virtues of two other members of the Finch family, both of whom passed away within three months of each other in 1627. One refers to Mrs. Elizabeth Finch, daughter of Sir Thomas Finch, "a gracious and truly religious gentlewoman," and the other to Lady Finch, "the virtuous and religious wife of the Hon. Sir Heneage Finch, Knight." At least one member of the noble family of Winchilsea shed his blood for his country, for the register denotes that Lord William Maidstone was slain aboard the Royal Charles, commanded by Sir John Harman, on June 1st, 1672, in a fight against the Dutch, in which the English were assisted by the French. His heir, Lord Charles Maidstone, was born posthumously on September 26th, to quote the entry in the register "at 9 a.m." The next successor to the title, Lord Thomas Maidstone, died on January 19th, 1695, almost a centenarian, he being in his 98th year at the time of his demise. A peculiarity is to be noticed in the manner of spelling surnames of persons commencing with the letter F, the ff as in Ffinch being used in every case from 1541 to 1645, when the use of the double letter was dropped. Referring to the burials of members of the Winchilsea family a curious reference is found. It is to the effect that the body of the Countess Katherine, who died from smallpox in London, was brought to Eastwell on May 8th, 1679, and buried "about 12 of the clock on Thursday night." Several entries notify cases in which persons buried in the churchyard met with unnatural deaths. One Thomas Bridges, we discover, hanged himself on March 4th, 1587, and was buried the same day; another, named Richard Brooker, was a madman belonging to Speldhurst, Sussex, and met an untimely end on December 13th, 1781. Then we find that on July 30th, 1551, three bricklayers named William Duffolde, Sampson Maywade and Thomas Pett met their death as the result of an accident, the nature of which is not given, and all were buried on the same day; William Ffarley, an aged man who was found drowned in a pit "by casualty," was interred on October 14th, 1611; and Robert Tocke, servant to

Lady Maidstone, who was drowned in a well at Boughton Lees on February 9th, 1626. Here and there are records of the burial of unknown persons who died in the parish. One was "a proctor and a poor man;" another a "blackemoore;" a third, "a young man who came sick to the parish and died here;" a fourth, "a stranger whose name we know not;" and a fifth, "an anonymous person found dead in a barn." There are many references to the death of indoor and outdoor servants at Eastwell House; several to "Oulde Mothers," and "Oulde Fathers," probably meaning aged widows and widowers; one records the fact that the son of John Heenan who died in infancy in 1568, was "lawfully christened by the testimony of divers sage matrons;" and another the death at the close of 1627 of Edward Hills, "a stone cutter of Boughton Monchelsea, died here in the Countess of Maidstone's work." Other peculiar references are to William Lea, "a soldier of the Low Countries;" Robert Myllis, "soldier and stranger;" John Manwode, "a young stroller out of Eastwell Place;" John Mason, "who died suddenly on the top of a load of hay;" Elizabeth Page, "a traveller;" Agnes Sharpe, "a maiden of 40 years old;" and Richard Thorpe, "an ancient householder." An entry against the date August 15th, 1707, intimates that on that day "Titherton, gooddy," was buried, and one can only conjecture that "Titherton" was an infant unnamed beyond the suggestive sobriquet of "gooddy." It is interesting to note that the whole of the twenty-four entries under the letter "O," covering a period of 169 years, refer to members of a family of the name of Ottaway, but this record is beaten by a family named Andrews, whose burials extend over a period of 264 years, and another family named Quested who resided in the parish for at least 203 years.

Burials of members of the Finch and Finch-Hatton families can be traced from 1552 to 1823, a space of 271 years. It is not generally known that the keeping of parish registers was made compulsory on September 29th, 1538, and there are in existence 812 registers, including that at Eastwell, which commenced in that year, and only eight whose entries are of an earlier date. Some interesting information can be culled from the Eastwell records. In order to encourage the woollen trade it was ordered in 1666 that all corpses should be buried in woollen shrouds or wrapped in wool, and affidavits respecting such interments had to be made before two magistrates. The first "woollen burial" appearing in the Eastwell register is that of William Sprat, interred on April 11th, 1682, and "allowed by Norton Knatchbull and C. Honywood," both of whom will be recognised as members of ancient Kentish families, representatives of which are still on the magisterial rolls. Other well-known names of magistrates who signed the Eastwell woollen book include Granville Wheler, J. Sawbridge (an ancestor of the family of Erle-Drax, of Olantigh Towers), E. Dering, Thomas Knight, George Sayer, George Carter and J. Toke. A fine paid to the poor was exacted whenever there was an exception to this order, and we find that this was the case in the burials of seven members of the Finch and Winchilsea families. Another interesting fact that is recorded is the charge of 3d. made for registering every marriage, birth, or death; this came in force at Eastwell on October 2nd, 1783. Ten inhabitants of the parish in 1671 subscribed £1 9s. 1d. towards the redemption of the Englishmen captured by the Turkish pirates on the coast of Morocco, and on August 7th, 1815, £33 2s. 6d. was raised for the sufferers "at the glorious battle of Waterloo." The register is made unique by the fact that it contains the original copies of the protestation against popery and popish innovations made in 1642; the vow and covenant to oppose and resist "the wicked and treacherous design to subvert the true Protestant reformed religion," (1843); and the solemn league and covenant "to preserve the reformed religion of Scotland, England and Ireland," to endeavour to exterminate popery, to preserve the rights and privileges of Parliament, the liberties of the three kingdoms and the King's person and authority in the preservation and defence of the true religion and liberties of his Kingdoms, to endeavour to discover all who would hinder the reformation of religion, the division of the King from his people or one of his kingdoms from another, to remain conjoined in a firm peace and union to all posterity, and to defend all entering into the league and covenant (1643). The first is signed by 28 persons, the second by 32, and the third by 19. A peculiarity in the signatures are the marks made by those who could not write. Instead of the simple cross made nowadays by an illiterate person, a rough attempt was made to write the first letter of the surname, but the marks resemble so many hieroglyphics. The writing owing to the use of abbreviations and contractions and the indistinctness is so difficult to read that in many cases a magnifying glass had to be used to decipher it. The register is further made notable by the fact that it appeared as documentary evidence before the Committee of Privileges at the bar of the House of Lords on June 5th, 1804, in a claim made by Lady Henry Fitzgerald and Sir H. Hunlock to the Barony of Ross. On that occasion two entries in the register—the burials of an infant child of Lord Winchilsea and of Diana, Countess of Winchilsea— were read. The baptismal records from 1654 to 1660 are very minute in detail. For instance, one is informed that "Sarah Martin, third daughter to Mr. Richard Martin by Frances, his wife, was born the 16th of April, 1659, on Saturday, about four of the clock in the afternoon and was baptised the 17th of the same, being Sunday." This looks as if the entries were recorded by someone who believed in casting a nativity in horoscope and thus preserved the exact time and date of birth. The registers of baptisms and burials are continued during the period of the Commonwealth—a very unusual fact—but the marriage register was not kept for about ten years of that period. During that time marriage was regarded as a civil contract only and was performed by a magistrate, banns being called in a public spot such as the nearest market place, while the nuptial ceremony was sometimes performed at a four- cross road! The register of births at present used contains the entry of the baptism of Princess Marie Beatrice, fourth daughter of the late Duke of Edinburgh, by the Rev. E. G. Gwynne, on May 17th, 1884. The only interesting facts to be gleaned from the old baptism register are the odd names given in olden days to infants. Thus amongst the masculine names are Rafe, Paris, Surtonlye, Cobblestone, Mosely, Ffaintnot, Ertzbargar, and Repent; while those given to females included Benedicta, Idenn, Thomasine, Alisia, Abigale, Everell, Richardine, Clemence, Abovehope, Bethulia, Posthume and Marable.

ELHAM.

———

STANDING on a sloping hill among much bigger hills is Elham. The valley which obtains its name from this old-world town runs between Folkestone and Canterbury, and as we pass through the villages that nestle in their midst we see on either side great rolling downs. They are but sparsely wooded; principally pasture land. The whole valley is but thinly populated, but as its picturesque scenery becomes known and the freshness of its air appreciated we are certain to see Elham and its neighbours go ahead to the tune of the builder's hammer. And there's the pity of it, you will say. The land everywhere is becoming over-built.

Elham! Yes, it sounds like a big place, for is there not the Elham Valley Railway, let alone Elham Board of Guardians and the Elham Division of Police? But as a matter of fact the tiny town merely lends its name to these public institutions. It is really no larger than a small village. Certainly it sends a guardian to look after the poor within its district, but the Elham Workhouse is in Lyminge, although the first meeting of the Board met at Elham on June 10th, 1835, under the chairmanship of Mr. Richard Jones. No less than four towns and two corporations are included in the Elham Union, but all bow their heads in point of name to the little town in the valley, even fashionable Folkestone and proud old Hythe.

Of course it was that scourge of our beautiful country scenery—the railway—which brought its name into notoriety. Years ago it was known as the Nailbourne Valley, but this was too old-fashioned a name for the railway director with his up-to-date notions, so he called the new line the Elham Valley Railway, and the old title is slowly dying away.

BRACKET ON "SMITHIES ARMS."

ELHAM FROM THE CHALK PIT

A CHARITY SCHOLAR

OLD MANTELPIECE AT "SMITHIES ARMS"

CORBELS IN THE CHURCH

MANOR HOUSE

X Willis

The strange name—the Nailbourne Valley—is derived from a remarkable cause. Through the valley, beside the railway, runs the Nailbourne, a stream which rises in a ploughed field near Sibton Park, on the high road from Lyminge to Elham, and runs in the direction of Wingmore Court, when it disappears in a flint pit known as "Old Mother Brompton's Pot." A mile further on it re-appears and runs towards Littlebourne. This spring, like all nailbournes, only rises every few years—once in seven years some old residents say. The volume of water from the spring differs at different periods. Sometimes it flows so strongly that the small bridges crossing the bed of the stream become too small, and the water consequently becomes in flood. But this is only on rare occasions, and the last time when it occurred was in 1877. Latterly the spring has failed to run—it has only risen once or twice since the construction of the Elham Valley Line—and this is attributed to several reasons. One is the sparsity of the rainfall in late years; another is that in cutting the railway at Each End Hill the spring was tapped; and a third is that the Folkestone waterworks in the Alkham Valley have diminished the supply. The word "nailbourne" is thoroughly Kentish, and is no doubt derived from the word "elebourne," and this has a connection with the abundance of eels which are found in the stream when it appears on the surface. I am told by one of the natives that he has even captured a three-pound trout—a proof that there must be abundance of water at times. In other parts of England these intermittent streams are known as winterbournes.

A strange and weird legend is connected with the Nailbourne. It dates back to the advent of St. Augustine in England, the year which was noted for a dry spring and a drier summer. As autumn drew near the land was in a shocking state from the drought. Trees and plants withered, flocks died from thirst. The opponents of Christianity at once proclaimed that all the trouble was the judgment of the gods upon those who had cast them off. Thereupon the Christian priests prayed for rain. But instead of rain miracles were performed. Upon the very spot where St Augustine knelt a spring of water bubbled up and ran along the country-side, moistened the dry roots of the grass, and instead of a parched barren waste a rich green hue spread itself all over the Elham Valley. Then came along Woden and Thunor, the heathen gods, and they stopped the course of the river by making great caverns underground, while sometimes they "dried up the waters by breathing on them with fiery and hellish breath." But the angel of the streams fought with Woden and Thunor, sometimes conquering, sometimes conquered. And still beneath the earth do they fight in their struggle for mastery. When the pagan gods are winning the Nailbourne ceases to flow, but when the good angels beat them down the stream runs clear and cool along the Valley. Judging from the experience of the past few years the guardian angel of the Nailbourne must be having a bad time at the hands of Woden and Thunor.

Up to 1825 the name of the village was spelt as it is pronounced, Eleham, and Hasted spells it in this way. There is a feeling amongst the inhabitants that it would be well if the old style were reverted to, for the present way of spelling is apt to cause much inconvenience to visitors, who invariably pronounced it like Pelham. Whence does Elham derive its name? The prevailing opinion is that it takes it from the large quantity of eels which were found, and are still found, in the ponds along the bed of the nailbourne stream; but another opinion is that its ancient name, Helham, denoted that it was situated in a valley among the hills. In Domesday the name is given as Alham. When we take into consideration the derivation of the word "nailbourne" as well as the old word "eleham" we can safely assume that the origin of the name, Elham, can be traced to its connection will eels.

In the old days you entered Elham by the road from Lyminge or Canterbury, and although it stands on a hill you come upon it suddenly. Now if perchance you ride, drive, cycle or walk along the Folkestone Road you can only get a glimpse of the church tower breaking through an otherwise clear horizon. You are quite close ere it dawns upon you that the town is near.

Nowadays, if you come by rail, you see the place standing high in front of you when emerging from the station. The old flint church stands out bold on your left as you mount the hill, but for a time we will leave it and pass round the corner and enter the ancient market square.

For Elham once was renowned for its market. Here came pedlars, here came stock dealers, here were brought hides from the neighbouring homesteads, when farmers fed on their own cattle; and it was for this reason that in the olden time the place was called the Leather Market. Some of the old residents can remember when a pleasure fair was held in the High-street, but all recollection of the market secured for Elham by Edward the First, when he was prince, in 1251, has entirely disappeared. At one time the privilege was kept up by holding a market once in five or six years, but even this practice was discontinued more than half-a-century ago. This ancient market, undoubtedly, was held in the Square, on the spot where we stand, and what was formerly the market house or shambles is now a row of cottages. When this market house was converted into cottages it was only on condition that a certain landowner erected a market cross to denote where the market was held, but the stipulation was, unfortunately, never carried out. Under the covered entrance, now converted into dwelling-houses, the lads of the town would congregate and play marbles and other games, while it was here that many of the present old ladies of Elham whiled away many happy hours in their girlhood with the skipping rope. Although no one recollects when the market-place was utilised for business purposes the oldest inhabitants do remember when on each Palm Monday an extensive business was done at the horse fair, and when the line of horses stretched from one end of the High-street to the other. As one good old soul, who has spent the whole of her eighty-three years in the village, remarked the other day, "That has been done away with a smart bit"—nearly half-a-century.

But before entering into the history of the old Square let us take a look around. As in other ancient villages there is no pretension to evenness of the ground. Why should there be? The vehicles that leave the centre track suffer no great harm, and even if the pedestrian suffer some slight pain to a tender foot he will bear it with composure rather than see the dear old squares and streets of his rural home macadamised, over prim, over neat. Around the market place are the cottages that now take the place of the old shambles; then there is the building that once did duty as a charity school; next we see the post office with its brick front dressed in ivy and clematis; at its side is the King's Arms, almost smothered in summer by trailing Virginia creeper; while on another side of the Square are houses covered in creepers—clematis and roses.

There are many things to talk about in this old market place, but they are things of long ago. The narrow thoroughfare leading out of the Square is known as Cock Lane, and it took its title from the former sign of the hostelry, which used to be the Cock Inn, now the King's Arms. The lane running to the station is termed Duke Street, but originally its title was Duck Street, this being taken from a duck pond close by. It may be interesting to state here that the churchyard wall bounding the road was erected under peculiar circumstances. The old one, which was much lower than the present wall, became so dilapidated that portions of it fell away, carrying in its descent part of the burial ground. Through the energy of the Rev. W. Wodehouse the flints for the new wall were given by farmers in the district, and the Vicar himself defrayed the cost of erection. Beyond the station the road leads up Running Hill to Swingfield and Denton.

The red house facing us as we look across the Square towards the street reminds us of two uncommon benefactions. One of them, the gift of Jonas Warley, D.D., was, until five or six years ago, distributed each Sunday after service in the form of loaves of bread, and the ancient custom was only deviated from when some of the recipients became too aged and infirm to walk to church. Originally (in 1722) a two-penny loaf was given away, then it diminished to a three-half penny loaf, but during the long incumbency of the late Rev. Walter Wodehouse the money was invested in the Savings Bank, and through his generosity it accumulated until it became possible to give each of the six widow recipients a quart loaf. By the other charity, left by Sir John Williams in 1725, a Charity School was founded for the instruction of six poor boys, "legal inhabitants, and born in the parish," in reading, writing and accounts. The testator also devised that the boys should be clothed once in two years, and when funds permitted one should be bound out apprentice. The testator's intentions are still carried out, and, curiously enough, the six boys are still provided with distinctive garb, which consists of velveteen knee breeches, coats like those worn by the Blue Coat boys, only slightly smaller, and adorned with brass buttons, sleeved waistcoats with similar buttons, which are worn without the coats in summer, blue worsted stockings and shoes, and blue pan-cake hat. Years ago this quaint costume was completed by a linen tie, the wearing of which, I hear, is likely to be revived. The worsted for the stockings used to be given to the lads' guardians, who had to knit them. A copy of the will of Sir John Williams is still in existence. One stipulation is that the six boys should learn to repeat by heart the Lord's Prayer, the Apostles' Creed, the Ten Commandments and the Church Catechism, and on every Sunday and holiday they were to attend at the parish church and repeat the same audibly to the minister before the congregation. The testator further devised that in the event of any of the boys proving "idle, disorderly or vicious" they were to be displaced in favour of others. The master's house stands at the corner of the Square, and it was here that the Charity School was carried on for generations. Now they are merged into the National Schools, which were built in 1844 and enlarged in 1871.

Around the church we will now take a stroll. From the railway station it has a stately appearance. An old bramble-covered tomb-stone with iron railings stands out grim and dark amid the bright white stones in the churchyard around it; the square, heavily but-tressed flint tower rises strong and massive in the west, while beyond is the quaint old street known as the Row, and yet higher still the grass-clad Downs. It is the tower that calls up our admiration, and when you walk round to its south side you will notice a remarkable growth of ivy, elder and other plants springing from the wall. No roots are visible; not even a trace of them. Far away, right in between the masonry, must they have burrowed. All we can see are their green shoots sent forth to meet the sun and grow strong and healthy under its genial rays. But, if we admire the grand old tower, a pang of regret escapes us as our eyes wander along the main building. The lead roof is mean in appearance, but worse still is the modern tile work in the south corner, utterly out of keeping with the rest of the edifice. If you mount the tower and look down from its summit you can see impressed upon the leaden roof the words, E. Prebble, I. Bailey, T. Bourn, R. Gilbert—church-wardens—1823. This denotes that this part of the roof was re-leaded at that time. On the roof of the south aisle are two more names over the date 1772.

This is not the original Elham Church that stands before us— the building that is mentioned in Domesday. That church disap-peared, no one knows how. Yet the present one is distinctly old, of Early English architecture. This is proved by the arcades in the naves. In two beautiful Decorated windows—those in the north wall, on each side of the porch—we have evidence of a later period. Other Decorated windows can be seen, one in the south wall of the chancel and one in the west wall of the north aisle. The idea of raising steeples seems to meet with public favour, but surely his grand square tower of Elham Church would look better with-out one! The present steeple superseded a smaller one when the bells were restored in 1887.

Now let us enter St. Mary's by the heavily-buttressed porch which is lighted by a narrow richly-coloured window of deepest tints. We open the inner door and at once become impressed with the sombre appearance of the interior. Yes, it is a sombre looking church. The black-stained pews make it so. Even the white walls, the red tiles of the floor and the white lights above fail to dispel the gloom. Perhaps the brightness caused by these latter make the black pews seem blacker still. But it is a fine open church, with plenty of room and high-pitched. The rugged simplicity of the timber ceilings are impressive. What changes these old wooden logs have seen!

The handsome Early English piers to the arcades are at once conspicuous when you enter the church. They measure over four feet one way and three feet another and are built of Normandy stone. There are arches on each side of the nave, while the chancel is entered under a fine wide arch, the latter being supported on one side by a bracket in the shape of a remarkable stone head, the tongue of the figure hanging out of the mouth. In the aisles we find more of these strange corbels, said to date back to the fourteenth century. So ludicrous are these faces that I defy you to look at one without smiling. The noses are battered, and this defect increases the oddity of their expression. The one in the south aisle is more perfect, but the pained look that evolves itself out of the chubby cheeks, the dilated nostrils and full lips makes it equally comical. The brackets supporting the labels of the windows are also in the shape of human faces, but the features are almost obliterated by copious coats of whitewash. What sins the whitewasher has to answer for!

There are several stained-glass windows in the church, but those which call for special mention are the two in the south chancel wall. One of them is the work of the late Mr. Frank Wodehouse, brother of the late Vicar. There are two lights, the subject of the first being "David playing the harp before Saul," and the figures portrayed are those of celebrities who were in the zenith of their fame at the time. King Saul is represented by Carlyle, at his side are the late Mr. Gladstone and the late Lord Beaconsfield, and in the second light is the present Premier, Lord Salisbury. The figures below are said to represent members of the Wodehouse family. The background of red and green is taken from a famous Italian painting. In the next window, which is the work of Mr. Samuel

Caldwell, of Canterbury, is an excellent likeness to the late Vicar, erected as a memorial of his ministerial jubilee in the parish in 1896. Writing of windows reminds me that when the church was restored a grand old Norman window was taken away from the west wall and replaced by the present lancet one. What shocking sacrilege! For, judging from an old picture, this window was immense, much wider than the present one. It is said that the cruel alteration was made so as to bring the window in keeping with the rest of the church. A weak, very weak excuse.

There are several other features of this fine old church to arrest your attention. Under the wall to the left of the chancel can be seen the remains of some beautiful old carving. It was a mediæval custom to place altars in the piers, and here at Elham we find the traces of such a shrine. It is a canopy of tabernacle work, elegantly carved, and traces of the paint can be distinguished. This reminds us that Elham Church is noted for its lights. In various parts of the interior can be seen brackets upon which images used to stand, and there is no doubt the lights were kept burning before these shrines, images and altars. No less than ten lights seem to have been in existence in the fifteenth century, and besides the money that was paid towards them by the living several legacies and bequests were left by those who died. To keep these candles burning and conduct the services regularly a large staff was necessary, and it seems from old documents that at one time two chaplains, as well as the Vicar and two parish clerks, were employed at the church. One peculiarity we notice in the chancel. Below one of the Wodehouse windows the sill is cut away so as to form a step, and upon this step it is supposed that the ringer of the old sanctus bell was wont to stand.

A visit to the vestry discloses a priceless treasure. Here, on shelf upon shelf, are valuable old books, including black-lettered specimens. This library was left by Dr. Lee Warley in 1809, and it is certainly a unique collection. Standing in the vestry is a wonderful old chest, the date of its make being the fourteenth century. It is hewn out of a solid piece of yew, with no pretension to symmetry, and evidently cut with the roughest of tools. Some idea of its heaviness may be gleaned from the fact that the lid is five inches thick in some places. In this lid are slits through which money could be inserted. Another old treasure, now alas! gone, was an ancient coffin slab which used to stand in the church porch, supposed by some to belong to the tomb of William de Elham, rector of Lyminge in 1313.

The organ in the church, the gift of members of the Wodehouse family, was erected in 1854 or 1855. It superseded an orchestral band, the members of which played in the gallery that formerly stood in the west end of the sacred edifice. The present pews were erected in 1846, also through the munificence of the Wodehouse family, and they succeeded old-fashioned high-backed sittings.

The eight bells in the belfry were all made in 1763 by the celebrated firm of Lester and Pack, of Whitechapel, the founders of the 70cwt. bell in Canterbury Cathedral, and were restored as a memorial of the Queen's Jubilee in 1887. It is nearly thirty years since the chimes in the parish church belfry resounded through the quaint old Market Square. They were placed in the tower when the clock was provided, but for a time they were silent through being out of order. However, Mr. Samuel Edward Dunn, who carried on the business of a watchmaker, re-set the chimes on the oak barrel, which, with many of the iron spikes still attached, can still be seen in the garden at the rear of the post office. The chimes played every four hours and ceased when the new clock was provided in 1873. Yet the old chimes could be heard for many miles around, and the effect, as the mellow sound echoed and re-echoed from hill to valley, and valley to hill, was delightful.

Lyminge shares with Biddenden the distinction of possessing one of the two first Communion Cups made in Kent for the use of the laity in the year 1561.

Before leaving the subject of the church I should mention that one of the Vicars of Elham, the Rev. Thomas Thompson, who held the living from 1761 to 1763, was one of the Six preachers at Canterbury Cathedral, and apparently had a peculiar experience as a missionary. It is recorded that he went to Africa, but "with all the pains he took" he found that he could be of no service to the natives of the Dark Continent. Consequently he returned to England, and was nominated by Archbishop Cornwallis to the living of Elham, where he passed the rest of his days with more success, let us hope, amid a white flock. Another vicar, Thomas Bradley, at the close of the fourteenth century, had a quarrel with his parishioners, the point in dispute being whether he or they should provide the holy water-stick or sprinkler for the church. Evidently the laity had the best of the argument, as the Vicar resigned in 1400.

Just out of the churchyard we come to a gate-way of old-world appearance in spite of its new green paint and whitewash. It is the entrance to the Vicarage premises, improved by the present incumbent, the Rev. Alard C. de Bourbel, and by its appearance suggests and in a clever way leads up in idea, so to speak, to the house itself, standing some thirty yards within. Pretty peeps of the house can be obtained from between the big gates and the wide archway overshadowing them, but the pedestrian enters by a small postern door, and immediately comes into full view of a truly picturesque house. It is small and cosy in appearance; long and low, with an old red-tiled roof, a bold white cornice, green-framed leadlight casement windows, rough white-washed walls, a sheltering penthouse, and a plain, yet massive, oak door. But all so thoroughly simple and homely. The interior is in thorough keeping; a hall, with a beautiful moulded oak hood to a fire-place surrounded with blue Dutch tiles; a long low-pitched living-room, with deep-set oak window seats and oak panelling, boldly moulded, entirely covering the wall, in the midst of which is the wide open hearth, whereon blazes that most comfortable of fires, logs of wood resting on fire-dogs. But yet another special feature of the interior must not be omitted—a well-staircase, entirely of oak, almost severe in its plainness and massiveness, yet lending a wonderful charm to the wide landing and passage upstairs.

Having looked round the church and buildings in its vicinity, let us now saunter up St. Mary's Road, on the right-hand side of which stands a building, with its boarded walls, once used as a brewery. Coming into the open we find the Street spreading itself to our view. As we face it in a northerly direction we note behind us the main entrance—the road which you traverse when coming from Lyminge. This road is a new one, as in the old days the town was entered by the Row—the main thoroughfare between Folkestone and Canterbury—and the present entrance was blocked, save for an alley which led into Vicarage Lane. It was at the side of this alley that the stocks stood.

Looking up the Street we see on our right the old hostelry, the Rose and Crown, with its new white face of stucco, while opposite is an older inn still, a long quaint building with hideous wooden faces peering from under the eaves. Further along the wheelwright's shop juts out into the road, the sign of the New Inn dangles on our right, pears hang in profusion from the fronts of houses on each side of the way—for it is September—and the blood-red Virginia creeper brightens the view; the white front of the Wesleyan Chapel rises above the dwelling-houses, and the road loses itself in the distance among the trees of the Canterbury road. Through the spaces betwixt the houses on our left we catch a glimpse of many chimney stacks that denote dwellings higher up the hill, and if you follow the lane leading to the old manor house you will come to another road known as the Row, built above the level and likening itself to the battlements of an old fortified town.

The Rose and Crown has a modern front, but its history dates back many years, and the old herring-bone brickwork of its walls denotes its venerable age. Here it was that the magistrates used to sit once a fortnight to administer justice. The Court was held in a long, narrow, upstairs room, with sloping ceilings on either side, which is now used as a private sitting room. The magnates sat at one end, and were divided from the rest of the Court by means of a moveable barrier. Attempts were made to remove the petty-sessions from Elham to Hythe, possibly for the convenience of the magistrates, with the result that the fortnightly sitting gave way to a monthly court, then to a quarterly court, and at last to a meeting of magnates once a year on licensing day as at present.

We now walk across the road and come to the old building which possesses no name. Many have been the surmises as to its origin, but the most plausible explanation is that it was an inn. Its very position and general appearance point emphatically to this assumption, while an old mantel-piece inside contains a panel, on which is painted the following :—" Richard Hayes. The Smithies' Arms. 1614." Obviously Richard Hayes was the landlord of the hostelry known as the Smithies' Arms. This old mantel-piece is a wonderful piece of oak carving, and the room in which it stands was probably the hall. The beam is bold and deeply carved. In the centre is an angel, on either side crouches a beast of the dragon species, with both tongue and tail spear-shaped, while at the outside corners are representations of a whale, from the mouth of which a frightened little Jonah is just escaping. Further scriptural subjects adorn the panels, such as the raven visiting Elijah in the Desert, the Temptation in the Garden of Eden, the Evil Spirit appearing before Eve in the guise of an ape, and the Dove returning to the Ark. In the centre is the coat of arms—the Smithies' Arms—

and the date 1614. Coming to the outside of the old house we see some marvellous carved brackets supporting the roof—figures exhibiting horrible contortions, with inhuman limbs. Here is one evidently intended to be a woman, there is a man with a long beard, and yet another with a close cropped beard, and some are shaven save for a ferocious moustache. At one corner is the body of an animal with breasts, the head of a man, and wings thrown back; at the other corner of the building is a mermaid, but the arm and hand with which she curls her tresses strangely enough are twisted round the wrong way. Altogether it is a wonderful collection—the weird work of a madman. The house itself is built of brick with plaster front, and a large sloping roof runs down to the back. It is now divided into four tenements, in one of which is some fine oak carving, and the property belongs to a member of the Bowes family. There is a local tradition which says that fabulous sums have been offered for the old mantel-piece inside, but I can find no reliable confirmation of the report.

If we follow the lane by the side of the old house we see Elham manor house at the top. This road, by-the-bye, is called Culling Hill, from the name of a family who occupied the manor house for many years. A timber and plaster building, this old house is by far the most picturesque in the place, and in course of time has passed through many hands, and has eventually come into the hands of the Papillons, the present lords of the manor. Once the owners were the Williams family, who were descended from the English family of Williams in Tallyne, in Breconshire. Thomas Williams, M.D., of Elham, was physician to Charles II. and James II., and was created a baronet in 1674. Sir Thomas Williams served in Parliament for Weobley, Herefordshire, and purchased in 1681 the Manor of Elham with the Manor of Ladwood. He married the daughter of Sir Edward Sawyer, of Woodbine, and had by her a son, Sir John Williams, Bart., M.P. for the county of Hereford. Colonel Symonds sold the Elham property derived from his great grandfather, Sir Thomas Williams, to Sir Thomas Oxenden, and the Manor of Ladwood to the Papillons, of Acrise Park. The Ruxtons of Brenchley are related to the Symonds, who at one time owned the Elham Manor. There is a panelled room and the front door is very ancient, but otherwise there is no special feature about the house.

In this direction is the Police Station, a building erected some thirty years ago. When the peace of the village was kept by the solitary parish constable there used to be a gaol on the site now occupied by the girls' school. The building was square in shape, and its ruins disappeared half-a-century ago.

Talking of modern buildings reminds us of the Institute, a corrugated iron building on the roadside as Elham is entered from Lyminge. Together, with the site, it was the gift of the Rev. W. Wodehouse and members of his family, and was built four years ago. Old foundations have been found on the ground attached to the Institute, and it is probable that this was the spot where the Earl of Ewe, who held the Manor of Elham in the 13th century, erected a magnificent palace. Many excavations have been made to discover more of this old palace, but nothing but parts of the foundations can be found.

Although not lying directly in the old Roman highway (Stone Street) Elham was no doubt frequently visited by the legions marching to and fro. Roman ornaments have been dug up, a silver coin of Hadrian was found in the Vicarage garden, another of the Empress Faustina beneath the floor of the church and a brass of Trajan in the same spot. Roman pottery has been discovered at Little Breach, between Barham and Elham, while at Wingmore a vase was unearthed. At Ottinge Farm is an old Roman burial place. Coins of a later period are frequently found in the town. One of the most valuable is a mediæval brooch of the 12th century in the possession of Mrs. Smith, of the Square. It was dug up in a meadow some few years since, and exhibited by the Royal Society of Antiquaries in London in 1878. In the centre is an antique gem, the subject of which represents a faun extracting a thorn from the foot of another faun. Around the brooch is the inscription, "Amor Vincit Fortitvdinem." At the back is a hoop for suspension, a hinge for the acus and a catch to hold the point.

But we have wandered from the Street. You naturally notice the handsome Wesleyan Chapel, erected in 1839, for Wesleyanism at one time was very strong in Elham, possibly on account of opposition to compulsory rates. The levying of such a rate led to some stormy scenes at the vestry meetings, and it also engendered bad feeling. The rate ceased between forty and fifty years ago, but it was some time before voluntaryism sufficed to enable the rate to be abolished. The peculiar little burial ground in front of the Wesleyan Chapel originated from this animus against the ecclesiastical tax. Two village Hampdens, by name Gillman and Johnson, were so embittered against the Church that before their demise they requested that their remains should not be laid to rest in the churchyard, and the vacant plot facing the old Wesleyan Chapel was converted into a miniature cemetery. What is known as the new Wesleyan Chapel was erected in 1839, and is a massive square building. On one side stands the old place of worship, now utilised as a Sunday school, and on the other side are the old Wesleyan day schools which flourished for thirty or forty years and have been converted into two dwelling-houses. No one who walks through Elham can fail to notice the quaint burial ground—one of the smallest in England I should think, for there are only four graves. And no room for more! The dates of the burials range from 1852 to 1861.

Just opposite can be seen two old cottages. One, according to the deeds, was originally known as the Barrack House, and before being rebuilt was a three-storeyed building, with old lead lattice windows. The thatched cottage adjoining was called the Butts, but why these appellations were attached to the property is unknown. Possibly they were connected with the concentration of troops in this part of the county to meet the threatened invasion of England by Napoleon the First.

The population of the town was 841 in 1801; now in 1901 it is 1,218.

One of the declined industries of Elham was rope-making, the walk being situated opposite the Wesleyan Chapel in the Cherry Garden Meadow, and last carried on by a man named Keeler about sixty years ago. Here it was that ropes for bells and agricultural purposes were made at the time when agriculturists grew flax and had to rely upon the village rope-maker for their ropes. But, like many other rural industries, it decayed with advancing times and town competition. Soap boiling was also carried on in the good old days in a building in High-street, situated opposite Mr. Gibson's establishment, and in recent years brick-making was conducted on a somewhat extensive scale and under rather peculiar circumstances. Although the bricks were made close to the railway station the clay was dug and "puddled" at Exted Farm, on the high land above the Row, and this was run by gravitation through pipes to the spot where the kilns are still to be seen below Cock-lane, in order that the bricks when made should be close to the railway station. The discovery of smelting pots and iron ore at Exted Farm leads one to believe that the iron smelting industry flourished in the district in by-gone days.

Up to about thirty years ago there were two windmills in the village. One, an old post mill, stood on the hills above the line, and this no doubt gave the heights the name of Mill Downs. This structure came to grief one stormy night, and the next morning its ruins were found lying in confusion in the meadows. The second mill stood on the site of the present one above the Row, and it was destroyed by fire about seventy years ago.

The old manor pound only disappeared about three years since. It stood close to the school play-ground, and its walls became so ruinous that it was thought advisable to demolish it altogether. The site is now occupied by a tree.

Elham Park, which was once an open demesne, is now nothing but a large thick wood, which stretches as far as Barham. The village possesses no seat or residence of any importance, the nearest estate being that of the Mackinnons at Acrise.

The name of Elham has for a great number of years been associated with coaching and hunting. From Folkestone to Canterbury, via the Elham Valley, is a favourite coaching route, and it is at Elham that the kennels of the East Kent Foxhounds are situated. The baying of hounds reminds you of this fact. The buildings are of comparatively recent date. Fifty years ago they were at Underhill, between Newington and Seabrook, and when Mr. Frederick Brockman succeeded his brother at Beachborough he built new kennels. This was some forty years ago. Lord Guilford then took the hounds and erected kennels at Waldershare, but when he relinquished the mastership the pack was located at Elham and has remained there ever since. The master now is Mr. Selby Lowndes.

FREELY·YE·HAVE·RECEIVED

ALMS BOX IN CHURCH

SAXON WINDOW

St ETHELBURGA'S TOMB

CARDINAL MORTON'S TOWER

St EADBURG'S WELL

LYMINGE.

ROUD in the possession of one of England's oldest
churches—"The Mother Church of England" it has been
called—Lyminge until a short time ago was a very
quiet, modest little village lying in the Elham Valley.
I say until recently, because of late years the builder
has been at work, outsiders, so to speak, have made a raid upon
it, and in every direction villas are taking the place of cottages,
red brick and tile the place of thatch and plaster, and the green
fields of the surrounding hills are becoming dotted with bungalows
and trim gardens. Yes, old Lyminge, the little place that was wont
to shelter itself only under the shadow of its venerable church, is
extending its area in all directions. But not only that. Old dwellings are being pulled down and new ones erected on the same
sites. A man returning now to his native Lyminge would scarcely
recognize the place. What a pity to destroy the old landmarks
some would say. But it so happens that in this instance there was
nothing of historic interest, nothing picturesque even in the cottages
that are gone. Strange that with this most ancient of churches
standing close by, not a single other building near is really old.
There must have been some houses years ago, but no traces remain.

Of more recent objects of interest we have plenty to talk about,
and an aged inhabitant, with a memory that even a younger man
envies, tells of the days when the first of the three Wesleyan chapels
in the village was built; when the stocks were used; when the parish
relieved its own poor—a much better way than the present poor
law system, he added parenthetically; when psalms put into meter
took the place of hymns at Divine service; when the village musicians sat in the church gallery and led the singing with the 'cello
and clarionette; when the present rich pasture land was for miles

around used as fields of golden corn; when the constable and "borsholder" kept the peace of the village; and when eightpence had to be paid for a letter from London. Yes, it is impossible to spend an hour in any village now-a-days without being struck by the changes of recent years.

But to our saunter through Lyminge. The church, of course, first arrests attention. It is prominently situated on a hill, almost hidden by majestic trees, and looks down like a sentinel upon the village below, houses and cottages closing in almost against its boundary walls. The solidity of the church at once impresses you—the massive square tower, embattled and surmounted on the north side by a fine turret, the deep-set walls that no weather could injure, masonry that has lived through many centuries and looks like standing till the end of time. The evenness of the stones of the oldest part are noticeable and arouse our admiration of the masons of long ago; but on the other hand the ugly little slated steeple raises our indignation against the taste of more modern architects. Why these unsightly additions to grand old towers? Fortunately all the ancient work is not spoilt. There are four old Saxon windows—one over the porch, one on the south wall of the chancel, and two on the north. Small they look compared to the modern Perpendicular windows. More like the loopholes of a stronghold, some might say. But to the antiquary they are priceless gems. Next we notice the huge flying buttress springing out at one corner, and no doubt placed there for the purpose of support rather than ornament. But it answers the two purposes. Its foundations are of Roman work. Further along the pathway and you come upon a mass of strange-looking ruins. They are all that remain of a noble building, historic since the days when Christianity first entered the hearts of our pagan forefathers. It is in these old ruins that most of the interest in Lyminge centres.

The story of the old foundations is practically the history of the church, and I cannot do better than give an outline of the career of St. Ethelburga, saint of Lyminge. It as a pathetic story. Ethelburga was the daughter of King Ethelbert and married Edwin, King of Northumberland. In her maiden days the young bride had been converted to Christianity and by care and love eventually persuaded her husband to join the ranks of the new religious community. But he paid the fullest penalty. At the Battle of Heathfield he fell, and thousands of his followers were likewise put to the sword. His young widow could only find safety in flight. She came down to her native Kent, and Eadbald, her brother, in a fit of compassion, gave her the park of Lyminge and here she settled down with her only daughter and two step-sons. The veil was her solace, Archbishop Honorious accepting her vows in the year 633. A long time ago. And yet we find even details of the fact handed down to posterity. This is explained by the fact that Ethelburga's trusted chaplain, who also fled after the martyrdom of Edwin, has placed the history of these bright days on record. For although sad to the poor young Queen, the events of those days were the brightest for Christianity. Not only did she found a nunnery and monastery in Lyminge, but by her pure and generous life caused the old Saxons of the district to see that the new religion was synonymous with goodness. The foundations of this ancient nunnery—the first founded by the Saxons in England—and this monastery—the second built in England, Folkestone possessing the first—are those we now see before us in Lyminge churchyard. They were built by Ethelburga upon still older foundations, so that it can safely be asserted that in this East Kent village lies some of the most ancient work now to be found in the British Isles. But the buildings suffered. The Danish invasion rendered the position of both the nunnery and monastery extremely dangerous, so early in the ninth century the former was removed to Canterbury, and the latter followed in its wake in 965. St. Dunstan thereupon restored the church, and the present chancel and south wall of the nave are the work of this period, the old materials being used—as evidenced by the Roman bricks, which we can see dotted about the remarkable masonry. Parts of the present south wall are built upon the old North wall of Ethelburga's church. The bones of the saint, as well as those of her niece, Mildretha—who succeeded her as abbess—were in 1085 removed to Canterbury by Lanfranc, and it is this open tomb which was discovered at Lyminge by Canon Jenkins not many years ago. It should be added that Lanfranc thoroughly restored the church in the eleventh century, having recovered the land from Odo, Bishop of Bayeaux, who with his accustomed greed had taken it into his keeping. Time went on and once more the church evidently got into a very bad state, for we find that in 1281 Archbishop Peckham thoroughly and carefully repaired it, adding the chancel arch and the flying buttress. Yet again, in 1382, exactly a century after, Lyminge church was restored, Archbishop Courtenay bringing stones from his various manors for

the purpose. The greater number of these stones, however, were devoted to the strengthening of Saltwood Castle. Twenty years went
by, and then the rector, William Preeve, built the eastern part of
the north aisle, but Cardinal Bourchier completed it in 1485, and
built the arcades, and for this reason it is now called Bourchier's
aisle. The erection of the present massive tower was commenced
by Cardinal Morton in 1495, and completed during the rule of Archbishop Warham.   For this purpose there seems but little doubt that
the ruins of the basilica were used as a quarry, and it will be
noticed that the stones at the top of the tower walls are larger than
those at the base.   This peculiarity arose through the smaller top
stones of the basilica being used first and the larger ones nearer
the foundations towards the finish of the work.   As a matter of
fact masonry of the following periods—Roman, Saxon, Norman, and
thirteenth, fifteenth and sixteenth centuries—is to be found at
Lyminge.

It will be seen that from its birth Lyminge church has been
looked after with loving hands. But there is even more to add. The
late Canon Jenkins was an ardent antiquarian, and during the time
he held the living unearthed the relics of the past—the old foundations
which we now see. Unfortunately his predecessor was too practical.
Discovering masonry beneath the surface he had it excavated and used
the material for the repair of neighbouring walls and lodges. It was
owing to this thoughtless action or ignorance that so much of the old
foundations have disappeared. For what remains we have to thank
Canon Jenkins. The present rector, the Rev. R. D. Eves, M.A., upon
being preferred to the living, at once set on foot a movement to
secure the complete renovation of the church. The work occupied the
best part of the year to complete, and during the time it was in
progress services were held in the adjacent National Schools.
Altogether the expenditure amounted to £1,807 10s. 5d.

Having followed the history of the present church let us now inspect
the remains of St. Ethelburga's basilica and tomb.   They lie in the
south side of the church in the vicinity of the porch. A basilica
is practically a Roman public hall, and the word is used in connection with the early Saxon churches of England which were built
upon the Roman plans. The ancient flint foundations at Lyminge are
open to view, and notwithstanding the necessity of bridging it by a
footpath the semi-circle can be traced without a gap. The tomb in
which the body of St. Ethelburga used to lie can easily be distin-

guished close to the church wall, and is denoted by a modern stone and inscription. If we follow the foundations of the wall of the old basilica we find that they continue parallel with the church wall in a westerly direction, until they reach the apse. An opening in the wall near the porch is a part of the entrance to the earlier church, which was apparently built much lower than the present one. Still working towards the west we find a hollow not far from the tower full of other ruins. These are the foundations of the apse, and close by its side can be traced the flight of steps.

Before entering the church it is worth one's while to look at the churchyard wall, which runs by the side of the flying buttress. It is modern at the top, but peer over the side and you will notice some grand old masonry. This was the original wall that enclosed the sacred precincts. The churchyard, by-the-bye, is remarkable for its size, while it has been in use for many centuries. The numerous head-stones to the memory of members of the Hogben family at once strike the visitor, and these are to be found even in the oldest part of the churchyard. In one corner, west of the church, is a memorial, "to parishioners and strangers who are buried near this place, to the glory of God, who gathered the outcast of Israel." This was placed there by Canon Jenkins, and is a thoughful memorial to those who ended their days in the workhouse, and whose remains were laid to rest close by.

Profoundly impressive is the interior of the church, which, by the way, is called "St. Mary and St. Eadburg." It is a spacious build-ing and its size apparently increased by the whiteness of the walls, which have recently been cleaned in the inner side, so as to show the marvellous evenness of the stone work carried out in the days of St. Dunstan. Entering the door we turn, and above us notice a small Saxon window, the deep red of the arch bricks standing out in bold relief against the white walls of stone. The small pieces of rich, coloured glass contain the arms of Cardinal Bourchier and were removed from the east window of the aisle when the organ was erected. The large window on our right as we look towards the door is an old one, and there are remains of Roman work—eight bricks showing that they are part of the original arch like the one over the doorway. Indeed there is no doubt that all the windows in the south wall were Saxon and of the same style as those which remain. The present large Perpendicular windows have ousted the little ancient ones. Glancing round the church we note the fine Tudor arch that gives entrance to the tower, and still farther along the three arcades of the same period. These arcades divide the nave from the aisle which was erected by Cardinal Bourchier. At the western side of this aisle can be seen part of the buttress of the earlier tower which used to rise from this corner of the church before the present one was built. The old tower fell down—struck by lightning, some say, but there is no evidence to prove it—and its masonry was utilised in the construction of the arcade.

The chancel is brimful of interest, and although the modern pews, the altar, the hanging lamps and the marble tablets on the walls bespeak more modern days, it requires but a faint stretch of imagination to see this part of the church in far-off days. The decisive depth of the clean-cut windows, the beautiful arches of Saxon work, the unique masonry of the walls relieved by a dash of red brick here and there like a splash of blood on a stone pavement, the old sacristy on the left, the large age-worn rafters above—all these belonged to years ago, so long ago that even if we know the date of the actual building no one can tell the age of parts of the masonry. There are now only three Saxon windows left, one to the south and two to the north, but until recent years there were four. One of them was taken away and superseded by a Perpendicular window, and, together with its neighbour, was restored a short time ago with stones taken from Elham church when the grand old Norman window of that edifice was sacrificed for new lancet windows. The large east window was erected in the sixteenth century, and it will be noticed how crude is the masonry, no attempt being made to join up the newer and older work with neatness. On the Maltese cross over the Communion table are the words, "Filiæ regum in caris tuis," somewhat bad Latin but literal Hebrew. They represent the text from the Psalms, "King's daughters were among thine honourable women," alluding to Ethelburga, who was a daughter of King Ethelbert. In the south wall, behind the pulpit, are the remains of an old altar, while directly opposite is an ancient stone coffin lid, standing up on end like a curiosity in an ill-arranged musuem, and decidedly out of place. The alms box hanging near the tower is a curiosity— nothing but a huge piece of oak opening halfway down, fastened with a padlock and having a slit in the top. Above it are the words, "Freely ye have received."

The church is rich in monumental tablets, which perpetuate the memory of members of the family of Honywood (of Sibton Park), Kelcey, Price (former patrons and holders of the living), and Jenkins. One states that Canon Jenkins, the venerable broad-minded rector and vicar of Lyminge for forty-two years, died on March 26th, 1894, having outlived his wife for the space of four months. Others give a touch of pathos in connection with the beloved rector's domestic life. Here we find that four of his sons died in far-off lands, two whilst serving their Queen and Country. Another tablet states that it was erected by Canon Jenkins to the memory of Henry Harvey Williams, who was for twenty years the master of the National Schools in the parish. Beneath the north and south chancel windows are to be seen two ancient brasses, bearing abbreviated Latin inscriptions. One denotes that Archbishop Dunstan restored the church in 965, and the other is to the memory of Thomas Duffin, priest, who was buried in the choir near the altar in 1508.

Formerly the vestry was situated beneath the tower, and over the tower arch at one time stood a gallery where the village musicians led the singing with wind instruments. In those days no hymns were used, only psalms set to metre being sung. The vestry is now behind the organ in a portion of the north aisle. The sweet-toned organ which superseded a one-manual instrument was the gift of the parishioners, and was meant to commemorate the 80th birthday of Canon Jenkins.

At present there are only six bells, and a visit to the belfry will convince you that the hangings are so far worn out that for safety alone it is necessary that the bells should be re-hung. Whilst speaking of bells it might be interesting to state that of the peal only two bear the same date. The oldest bell is the second, made in 1631. It bears the brief inscription, "Wilner made me, 1631," with the initials "W.M." added. The fourth bell dates back to 1727, and has inscribed upon it, "William March—Robart Wood—Sam Knight, fecit 1727." In 1759 the tenor bell, which weighs 18cwt. 97lbs., was made by Lester and Pack, of London, and it bears the name of Mr. Richard Kennett, churchwarden. The third and fifth bells were both cast by William Mears, of London, in 1785, and at the time Thomas Fordred and John Swaine were churchwardens. The treble is the most modern bell, as its date, 1810, denotes. This also came from Mears' foundry, and the names of William Sawkins and I. Cloake are inscribed thereon as being churchwardens at the time. There is a tradition that the smallest bell was cast in a field near the church and that silver coins were thrown into the molten metal by members of the Honywood family then residing at Sibton.

Lyminge, now in Elham Deanery, was at one time head of a rural Deanery. Stanford living was formerly held, together with Paddlesworth, by the Rector of Lyminge, and as long ago as the end of the 18th century efforts were made to make the benefices separate. Stanford is now a distinct living, but Paddlesworth remains attached to Lyminge.

Down from the church we walk into the village, a compact little place, all corners so it seems. It has three main entrances. One leads from Canterbury via Elham, a distance of about fourteen miles, another from Folkestone and Hythe, and the third from the Roman Stone Street road. Among the cluster of houses by the side of the last-named road stands the quaint post office, and close by we come to "The Yard"—a farmhouse fronted by a pond. This property comprised part of the Bedingfield benefaction. It was left by one Timothy Bedingfield, an affluent resident of Dymchurch. The trustees are empowered to apply yearly a sum not exceeding £15 in apprenticing deserving boys, who must, for not less than five years, have been in some public elementary school. The proceeds of the charity are derived from land at Lyminge, Smeeth and Woodchurch, and by his will, dated 1691, Bedingfield bequeathed this property towards the education and maintenance of children of the parishes of Smeeth, Lyminge and Dymchurch, together with 10s. yearly to two poor women—5s. each—in each of the three parishes. The benefaction board in the church says that the income is to be devoted to the education of poor children, frequent communicants, and who do not actually receive parochial relief; and also the sum of 5s. each to two poor women, after receiving the Sacrament of the Lord's Supper on Christmas Day. The apportionment is £23 6s. 8d. to each of the benefitting parishes, and the charity is under the care of nine Governors—three ex-officio, three representative and three co-optive. The first-named are the rectors of the three parishes; and the second are appointed in vestry. The first co-optive Governors appointed for life in 1882 were Lord Brabourne, Mr. William Deedes, Major George Deedes, Sir Wyndham Knatchbull, Sir J. W. Honywood and the Rev. R. B. Knatchbull-Hugessen. The terms of the Charity empower the Governors to "determine" any scholarship if the holder is guilty of serious misconduct or idleness, shall fail to maintain a reasonable standard of proficiency, or shall wilfully cease to pursue his or her education. And if there are no candidates qualified for examination the awards shall be competed for by boys or girls in any of the parishes adjoining Lyminge, Smeeth and Dymchurch, or any other parish named by the Governors.

One Charity lost to Lyminge parish is that of an almshouse in two tenements, left by an unknown benefactor. There is an old house to be found in the village bearing a tablet on which are the initials " L.P.," but whether this is the almshouse mentioned or not no one seems to know. Anyhow the poor do not at the present time receive any benefit from this benefaction. There is also a plot of land situated on the continuation of the Street, still known as " Shoe Land." In olden days it was no uncommon thing to find pieces of land left to parishes for the provision of shoes and other things for the poor, and these plots were always named after the nature of the benefaction. This was no doubt the case at Lyminge.

Not far from the Yard is a low, one storeyed building bearing a tablet on which is inscribed the date " A.D. 1830." This is the old workhouse, and by this name it is still known. At one time when the poorer classes could not find means with which to keep themselves the farmers had to employ them on the land, and keep them for what they were worth in labour. In some cases this would be avoided by a benevolent yeoman giving away gristing—corn or flour—then came the parish workhouse built through the liberality of a lady, who intended it to be not a workhouse but a home for the aged poor. But how different was the management of the poor in early days ! here at Lyminge the persons in charge of the poor-house—a happier name than workhouse—were a man and his wife, who, in return for looking after the inmates, lived in the place rent free.

If you follow the road towards Stone Street you come upon the original site of the Court Lodge—an undulating field west of the church. Here are all sorts of mounds, not old, but in many cases caused through excavations made by antiquaries in the hope of finding relics of the past. At the top of this field the old manor pound still stands. The ancient custom of calling the Court on the site is still observed. The present Court Lodge is about a mile from the church, and stands at the "four-went way" where the roads from

Postling, Lyminge, the Farthing and Each End Hill meet. Now the farm is called New Barn, and for a peculiar reason. Many years ago the homestead was burned down by a roving band of agricultural labourers, who were incensed at the occupier using machinery instead of labour. Fresh barns were built, and henceforth the name of the farm was known as " New Barn."

Returning to the heart of the village we see the new Wesleyan chapel, a fine building. The Wesleyan body at Lyminge dates back to about seventy years ago, and its progress is worthy of record. When the Wesleyans first established themselves in the village they had to encounter a good deal of opposition and bitterness, which in some instances amounted to persecution, but during the long ministry of the late Canon Jenkins Wesleyans and Episcopalians worked together in the most harmonious manner. The first chapel was erected in the Street close to the village forge, and is now used as a dwelling-house. The next move was made adjacent to the Station-road, and here again we find the old temple of worship doing duty as a habitable dwelling. The Society grew so strong in numbers that within ten years of its erection it became necessary to enlarge the building, and it then did duty until the present place of worship was opened in 1895. The burial ground attached to the second chapel is still retained, but interments have not taken place there for the last twenty years. Towards the cost of the chapel and the manse the late Mr. Thomas Rigden contributed munificently, and inside the building can be seen a tablet erected to the memory of this generous supporter of the church of his choice. The close of Mr. Rigden's long life came when he had lived to the age of eighty-five years. The house in which he died is five centuries old and has been occupied by members of the family for many generations. He was one of the world-renowned sheep breeders, and much of the wealth he amassed in his business was devoted to religious and charitable objects.

The mention of Nonconformity reminds one of the battles royal formerly fought in Lyminge over the church rates. While adherents of the Establishment favoured the tax Dissenters stoutly opposed it and the division engendered much bad blood. On the first day of March, 1855, some thirty or forty parishioners assembled at the vestry and adjourned to the hospitable roof of the Coach and Horses to discuss whether or not a church rate should be levied for the necessary repairs of the church, and "for such other purposes for which by law a church rate may be made." In the end a poll was demanded, with the result that twenty-seven voters registered in favour of the rate and twenty-one against, and by a plurality of voting it was announced that altogether forty-five votes were given for the rate and thirty-four against, making a majority for the rate of six voters, or eleven votes. In spite of the poll it appears that the rate was never collected, and henceforth the imposition of a compulsory church rate died out.

The village blacksmith's shop in the Street has been in the hands of the Hogben family for over a century, and has always been carried on by the family of that name. The end cottage of the row of buildings adjoining the forge, and which faces the inn, was at one time a smugglers' haunt, but that was many years ago; in fact, before the time of the oldest inhabitant. Upstairs in the roof can be seen a secret chamber in which the illicit goods were secreted.

The stocks formerly stood close to the entrance to the churchyard facing Mr. Baker's establishment, but, as is the case in the majority of villages, they were never preserved; they decayed, and many years ago disappeared.

Although possessing neither market or fair, Lyminge at one period presented an animated appearance at Michaelmas time. On Michaelmas Day the farm labourers, waggoners, mates and boys would assemble outside the Coach and Horses, and to the tune of the merry cracking of their new whips exchange the sayings peculiar to the men of the land. "Pork agin? or 'ow?" was the question addressed to each other with the object of ascertaining whether a situation was going to be retained for another year, or whether a change was being made. Jolly days were these. Gone alas! for ever.

The original part of the present schools dates back to 1849, and occupies the site of the previous village educational establishment. The buildings have been twice enlarged since that date, the infants' department being the latest addition. The schools receive handsome aid from the charities. The Bedingfield benefaction provides a grant of £23 6s. 8d. a year in scholarships. Then the schools get the benefit of the proceeds of the Kingsford Charity, by which a yearly sum of £10 arising from land in Lyminge and Paddlesworth was left in 1817 by the testator for the education of poor children of the two parishes mentioned.

By the side of the road leading up to the village is St. Eadburg's well, now covered by an oaken canopy bearing the date 1898.

E

Local tradition says that the supply never fails and at the present time it forms the principal source of the Little Stour. The parish records show that the well has been a public one for a long period. As long ago as 1484 one John Gardyn, a resident of Lyminge, left a bequest for its preservation, ''if the parishioners should be unwilling to undertake the work.'' Nine years later a member of the Dering family left money for its repair, and when the late Colonel Hony-wood, of Sibton, was Member of Parliament for the county, he built a well-house and dipping place. This dipping place was succeeded by the present chain pump. The waters of this ancient well supply not only the inhabitants of the village proper, but in times of drought residents in the hilly districts around come to the spring for water for themselves and their stock. The protection of the well is of such serious moment that in 1878 two ponds, one on High Minnis and the other on Rhodes Minnis, were sold, the proceeds invested in consols, and the income utilised in preserving the well and its supply. Eventually the consols were sold and the money devoted to the construction of the present well and pump. Speaking of the water supply, it is a remarkable fact that whilst at one time a large volume of water ran through the village from Each End Hill none is to be seen at the present time. For years the water sources in the valley have been gradually diminishing, but a good supply is about to be sent from waterworks now being erected close to the high eminence known as the Farthing, where, it might be added, is to be found the highest spot in East Kent—about five feet higher than the loftiest spot at Paddlesworth. At Each End Hill there is a parting of the water shed. One stream runs through Newington to the sea, and the other, the Eastbrook Stream, becomes a tributary of the Lesser Stour. But since the railway was constructed the water has not been up to its previous height, and undoubtedly a valuable artery of the source was either cut or diverted with the introduction of the line. Before the source of the Nailbourne was cut or other-wise affected the stream used to run freely in Sibton Park at the spot where the cricket ground is now situated. In those days the river, as the old inhabitants still love to call it, was full, and ran right into the Stour at Littlebourne.

There is but little history attached to the mill which stands at the end of the village close to the entrance to Sibton Park. It succeeded a former mill which was destroyed by fire about ten years ago.   For a long period the spot was occupied by two mills, one of which was black in colour, and the other—the present one— white.   It was the former that fell to the fiery element, but previous to the erection of either a post mill stood in one corner of the Sibton Park Estate, close to the bungalow residence on the road from the Street towards Stowting.   These post mills were in olden times familiar land marks in country parishes.   They were provided principally on estates before corn grinding became a business, and it was in the old post mills, built by the landowners, that the tenants on the various estates had their corn ground.   The one at Lyminge, like that at Elham, fell a victim to a heavy storm.   Long before the recollection of the present inhabitants a water mill stood by the side of the stream which flows from St. Eadburg's well, facing the station, and the level green field bordering the station road was then the site of the mill pond.   This in all probability was used by the general public who were not entitled to take their corn to the post mill.   The foundations of the old water mill can still be traced close to a bridge which spanned the stream.

Not far from the village stands Sibton in a beautiful park. Originally it was known as Sibeton Manor, held by the family of Fitz Bernard during the reign of Edward I.   Ultimately the estate reached the family of Hales, but during the reign of Queen Elizabeth Sir James Hales alienated it to a Salked, one of whose descendants left it to Mr. Nicholas Sawkins, in the possession of whose family it remained until 1786, when Mr. William Honywood bought it of Mr. Jacob Sawkins.   This Sawkins family was known in various parts of Kent, members of it residing at Egerton, Canterbury, Willesborough, Ashford, Maidstone and Margate.   One of them, John Sawkins, was town clerk at Canterbury, and—so strong must have run the legal blood through their veins—everyone of his three sons, John, Joseph and William, were attorneys in the cathedral city. Captain John Howard, M.P., the present owner of Sibton, purchased the property, which consists of 656 acres, from the descendants of Mrs. Philip Honywood, of Mark's Hall, about six years ago.   Captain Howard has always interested himself in the Royal East Kent Mounted Rifles and holds a commission in the regiment; as further evidence of his patriotism after the outbreak of the Boer war in South Africa he volunteered to serve his Queen and country at the front.   Upon returning to England he was elected unopposed as Member of Parliament for the Faversham Division of Kent.   As the

Hon. Mrs. Howard is the daughter of the late Lord St. Vincent and sister to Lady Harris the interest of the present owner of Sibton and his wife in county matters is naturally pronounced and the popularity of both in the district is great. In 1898 Captain Howard added a considerable number of rooms to Sibton and improved the domestic offices, at the same time building more stables and coach-houses, but the old part of the residence was not interfered with. Some three years ago a stone slab was found hidden away in a corner of the building, bearing the following inscription :—

1602.

N.S.		S.
		I. M.

The date evidently refers to the period in which the house was erected and the N.S. doubtless are the initials of Nicholas Sawkins. The meaning of S.I.M. cannot be determined. Captain Howard has had the stone slab carefully imitated and placed above the front door on the outside of the building. Longage Manor is attached to Sibton and here in the ancient farmhouse has been discovered some old oak wainscotting with the date 1608 burnt on it—probably the date of Longage manor house.

Robus Farm, the house of which is an old oak timbered building in an excellent state of preservation, takes its name from the Robus family who flourished in the village for many generations. It stands on the left-hand side of the road leading from the station to Elham.

If one cares to climb the rising ground at the back of the Work-house at Each End Hill, known as Brockman's Bushes, a moss-covered stone can be found in the middle of a meadow. Here it is that four parishes meet—Newington, Saltwood, Postling and Lyminge. Standing 597 feet above sea level you can look down upon the familiar spot at Beachborough known as Summer House Hill, and a grand imposing view can be enjoyed. Another curious fact is that the centre of the Stone Street road for a long distance divides Lyminge from several parishes. Lyminge is a long straggling parish, but extremely narrow. By going in the direction of Stelling Minnis we come to Wheelbarrow Town—a manufacturing town some cynics call it because the industrious settlers manufacture bobbins. It is, in truth, an out-of-the-world spot, and Hasted, in his description, says that the inhabitants are as wild and in as rough a state as the country they dwell in. It is here that much of the faggot firewood used at Shorncliffe Camp, and at Folkestone, Hythe and Sandgate is made, and this industry has been carried on at Wheelbarrow Town for generations. Men, women and children can be seen hard at work, both winter and summer, in low thatched wigwams cutting the faggot wood and tying it into bundles with hop-bines. Why it is called Wheelbarrow Town no one seems to know, but one individual suggested that it was because rows of men could once be seen trundling barrows, laden with bundles of wood, to the seaside.

In this vicinity is to be found a small burial ground. It is a triangular-shaped plot containing two yew trees and four headstones. There is no attempt to keep this God's acre sacred; the graves which cover the remains of the unknown and the headstones are grown over with grass, and beyond a straggling letter here and there nothing can be traced of the inscriptions on the stones. The history of the burial ground is totally lost.

At Each End Hill, in the further corner of the parish of Lyminge, and bordering on that of Newington-next-Hythe, stands the block of brick buildings known as the Elham Union Workhouse. The cleanliness and neatness of the institution, both inside and out, are a credit alike to the guardians and officials. When one beholds the practical work of the Poor Law system—although many individuals are apt to speak to its disparagement—one cannot help comparing it with the system of half a century ago. Instead of being of a prison-like character—the imagination of many of our elders at the present time —the workhouse of to-day provides a home for our more unfortunate fellow beings than they ever found in their humble dwellings. The pity of it is that the word "workhouse" is used; the old-fashioned "poor-house" is much better. Not only do the inmates have a sufficiency of good, plain, homely food, but they are all well clothed and well shod, in short, life here would surprise many who barely exist on a small pittance outside the friendly shelter of the workhouse roof. It is only the English characteristic of independence which keeps them away. It was some sixty or seventy years ago that by order of the Poor Law Commissioners the village poorhouses gave place to one large establishment for each Union district, and an old stone, still preserved, in the original front of the original Workhouse at Lyminge, denotes that the building was erected in 1835. This stone is now to be seen upstairs in the old men's dormitory. A special feature connected with the administration of the poor law in this Union is the institution of Cottage Homes at Cheriton for children, who are thus saved from the stigma which might attach to them in after years through having been reared in a workhouse.

Just a word about the Union district and its representatives. Elham Union comprises the parishes of Acrise, Cheriton, Elham, Elmsted, Folkestone, Hawkinge, Hythe, Lyminge, Lympne, Monks Horton, Newington, Paddlesworth, Postling, Saltwood, Sandgate, Folkestone-next-Sandgate, Sellindge, Stanford, Stelling, Stelling Minnis, Stowting and Swingfield. Of the 34 guardians, Folkestone contributes twelve, Hythe three, Cheriton and Sandgate and Folkestone-next-Sandgate two each, and with the exception of Newington and Paddlesworth, and Stelling and Stelling Minnis, which have each one between them, the remainder are represented by one member each. At one point the district covered by the Union stretches from Hythe to Stelling, a distance as the crow flies of some eleven miles; in another direction, from Folkestone to Elham, a stretch of ten miles; and in a third course, from Lympne to Swingfield, thirteen miles. Elham is the most extensive parish with 6,599 acres, and Stelling Minnis the smallest with only 81. In population Folkestone comes first with 30,209—nearly two-thirds of the whole population in the district—and Paddlesworth last with 49.

The past century has seen the population of Lyminge increase from 491 to 1,030, the great increase of recent years being accounted for by the village becoming a favourite spot for those seeking a quiet retired life—residential quarters for those who wish to escape from the hurly-burly of the towns and yet remain within easy distance of the sea.

THE LATTICED GATE.

FIREPLACE IN INNER COURT

A PEEP FROM THE GARDEN

AT THE LOCK.

IN THE DOVECOTE

THE ENTRANCE GATEWAY

X.Willis.

ALLINGTON.

———

A TINY parish—not a village, not even big enough to call itself a hamlet—yet full of historic relics—the relics of a grand old Castle—is Allington. It lies just outside the county town and yet no main road passes through it. You can take the Chatham road out of Maidstone and branch off down to the river when you reach Sandling; but the easiest and pleasantest way is to saunter along the Medway tow-path. Although very prosaic and practical there is always something picturesque about a tow-path. In the first place, a certain amount of fascination overhangs the waterside. The man of sporting proclivities is interested in the circles—small at first, then slowly widening—that form themselves upon the surface of the water. His knowledge tells him that fish are moving—maybe large pike, maybe small fry—but still they are of the fish tribe, and instinct makes him excited. There is the waterfowl that haunts all streams. And the overlapping trees, the graceful reeds, the wild flowers and mossy banks make the naturalist happy. To the artist a fine river like the Medway is always full of beauty. It is never monotonous. For just as the place seems silent and lifeless round the bend comes a heavy barge, drawn by stalwart horses or back-bent bargee, smoking or humming as he walks, giving a touch of colour, a touch of life to the scene.

This is what you can see as you walk to Allington, but if you would see the little place at its best mount the hillocks on the Boxley side of the river. Here at our feet runs the Medway, losing itself in the bend beyond the lock and the many tan-coloured sails of passing barges alone prove the commercial utility of the river without corroboration from the volumes of smoke which rise and begrim our view on the left, where asphalt works now stand. Just across the river, embedded in a band of willows, stands the castle, its white walls half covered by ivy. Uneven in height, relieved by many a tower—some dwarfed and decayed, some tall and one even roofed in—enough of the old building remains to show what defensive strength it once possessed. It guarded the river and the depth of its walls, encompassed by a moat, held any land assault in check. Smoke now rises from amid the ruins and tiled roofs that cap some of the masonry, showing that parts are inhabited still. On our right are the barns and oasthouses of a farmstead, half hidden among the trees, but no smell of drying hops ascends, only heaps of stones from a neighbouring quarry can be seen with which to laden the barges by the riverside. Away up the slope runs the woodland, entirely hiding the little church from view. Farther beyond, a trifle to our right, the horizon is cut by the grey outline of the distant downs that overhang Kemsing.

To cross the river we pass over the Locks. Up to this point the Medway is tidal, but not beyond. Originally it was tidal as high as Maidstone, and only a few years since were the old locks near All Saints' church removed. Barges, therefore, used to sail up to Maidstone with the tide. It was in the forty-second year of the reign of George the Third that the Lower Medway Navigation Company obtained their Act of Parliament, the Company being incorporated in 1792. The Act gave the Company powers to dam the river at Allington, make towing paths and render the river navigable, at the same time empowering them to levy tolls. Thus it would be towards the end of the 18th century that Allington locks first came into existence. Previously there existed a ford across the river opposite the lane which comes down from the Aylesford road and the road which runs up by the Castle. The present locks are made in the newest style, obsolete portions having been removed from time to time, and about twenty years ago they were lengthened.

It is curious to note that the parish of Allington crosses the river and runs up as far as Cobtree, the residence of Mr. Tyrwhett Drake, between the Chatham and Aylesford roads. Boxley parish comes right down to the river opposite the Castle.

A winding lane leads to the Church, small but beautifully restored and decorated, in the last instance two years ago. It is one of the smallest churches in Kent, but quite large enough for the population of the parish, 141 all told. The porch and tower are old, but inside everything is new. It is chastely decorated in Tudor style and every

Mr. Falcke has left Allington Castle, and the present tenant is Sir Martin Conway, the famous explorer, scholar and author, who has made many alterations since the description in this volume was written.

window is of rich stained glass.   The two east windows were erected to the memory of the Rev. G. F. J. Marsham (a former rector) and his wife in 1868.   In 1898 the three-light west window was erected in memory of members of the Hubble family, while in the same year the font was given by the sons and daughters of John and Amelia Holmes, in memory of their parents.   On the floor of the chancel is a tombstone recording the death of Sir Edward Austen, of Boxley Abbey, and his wife, who died in the years 1760 and 1772 respectively. Sir Edward was descended from Sir Robert Austen, formerly of Hall Place, Bexley.

Allington possesses no school of its own; the children trudge either to Maidstone or Aylesford for their education.

Traces of a Roman villa were found on the west side of Allington Castle in 1844 and at the same time it was discovered that the road leading to the old fortress had been repaired by pieces of Roman tiles. About a hundred yards away from the ruins of the villa in a quarry was uncovered a tile tomb.   The cist was formed by burning clay beneath as a floor, upon which the corpse was placed in a bed of moss.   Over this a dome was made with pieces of wood and above this frame-work was placed a layer of clay.   A fire was next lighted so as to burn the clay hard and thus form a hard ceiling or dome over the corpse.   The latter was found with the head bent forward over the chest and the knees raised.

Let us now stroll along the lane till we come to the gem of the place, Allington Castle.   Its former glories departed years ago, since when the ruthless hand of time was allowed full sway until the present tenant, Mr. Falcke, about six years ago came to the rescue and saved the old place from further decay.   For years it had been used as a farmhouse, while the site of the old banquetting hall was given up to heaps of rubbish, the outer bailey to the tender mercies of cattle and sheep, and the pleasance, now scented by the perfume of roses, trampled by swine.   A true lover of ancient relics, Mr. Falcke has spared no care to reclaim that which was lost, to repair damage without destroying the fabric and to stay decay.   No ugly new buildings pain the eye; the old have simply been repaired and preserved.

As for the history of its early days we are entirely dependent upon old historians like Kilburn, Hasted and Seymour, who themselves dipped into ancient records for information.   Seymour says the first castle was built by the Columbarii when they invaded these shores and that the

Danes afterwards demolished it. But we go back to Saxon times with more certainty to find that a house stood here, a fortified building probably, as in those bloodthirsty days of turmoil every habitation was its owner's stronghold, ready against attack. Its possession can further be traced to Ulnoth, son of Earl Godwin and Harold's young brother: then to Bishop Odo, from whom it was taken by William Rufus, owing to Odo's treachery, and given to Earl Warren. It was this nobleman who turned the place into a fine baronial residence. Next we hear of Sir Giles Allington living there and giving the name to the parish. But when it became the property of Sir Stephen de Penchester, governor of Dover Castle, that old soldier with military instinct obtained permission from his sovereign, Edward the First, to more strongly fortify the old moated house. Next one of the Cobhams held it and then another Kentish family, the Brents. From this family it was alienated to the Wyatts, two ill-fated members of which—the one a poet and the other a fiery soldier and revolutionist—met with an early death. After Sir Thomas Wyatt's execution Queen Elizabeth gave the property to her Master of the Jewels, one John Astley, and it was from his descendants that the Marsham family secured it, and at the present day it belongs to the Earl of Romney.

So much for the history of Allington Castle. Let us now look at it as it stands to-day, a ruin, but not ruined to such an extent as to bury all its past glories and leave them to tradition only.

Approaching the Castle by the gateway we notice a strong round building just outside the moat which is said to have been the old barbican. If it was, the moat must have been wider than now appears—the moat which now only runs partly round the Castle, some of it having been filled up within the last fifty years and an orchard planted on the spot. Towards the entrance—flanked by a round tower on each side—a gateway that reminds one of the entrance to Carisbrooke Castle—over a stone bridge we pass— not a drawbridge—that disappeared a long time ago—but there are relics of the old defensive works still remaining. The ancient gates are of massive oak with powerful hinges, their surface thickly studded with iron bolts and heavily latticed at the back. Battering rams may have worked their destruction in time, but the attacking force must run the gauntlet of point-blank firing from the loop-holes of the round towers on either side and from a large window over its very centre. Then again there was the portcullis, now alas! gone, but the grooves in which it rose and fell are clear to the light of day. The exterior walls of this gateway were erected in the thirteenth century, but the Tudor window in the centre and other Tudor masonry within the building show that the interior was re-built at a later date. On the right is the guard-room with a single cell at the back—a cell no doubt in which many a wretched prisoner groaned in his sufferings. It was a dismal hole, its darkness relieved with just a glimpse of light from a slit that pierced the wall. There is evidence of a room above, a Tudor mantelpiece in a splendid state of preservation defining its date; but the flooring has entirely disappeared.

Passing through the gateway the square court known as the outer bailey spreads itself before us, surrounded by high walls, over which vines and ivy now climb and struggle for supremacy, while traces of an inner wall can be seen on our left, probably the wall which originally supported buildings. Just at our feet is the very stone used for bear-baiting, actually on the spot where it originally stood. Facing us is a fine Tudor archway that leads to the inner court, and in the walls can be seen the "put-log holes" made for the support of scaffolding by the masons of old and never filled in. On our left is the Tudor porch which leads to the front door with the ruins of the banquetting hall close at hand; on our right is a flight of stone steps leading originally to the upper chambers through four Early English doors, having at their bases "dagger stops," which indicate the period.

Under the Tudor arch near by we stroll to the inner court, with the huge fireplace cut in its walls, large enough for the roasting of an ox whole. Although the buildings facing this court are more modern than other parts of the buildings—Elizabethan in fact—they make a delightful picture. From a corner of an inner court rises "Solomon's Tower," so called as far back as the time of the oldest chroniclers, though upon what grounds no one knows. It is the watch tower of the castle and was built by Sir Stephen de Penchester. From its summit, which can still be reached by stone steps though with a certain amount of risk, the valley of the Medway could be scanned for some distance, and an enemy discerned approaching by land or water. "Solomon's tower" has been described as the keep, but it so happens that Allington Castle was one of the first in England to be built without one. In the tower are the remains of a big hooded fireplace.

Roaming about the grounds we find that the best view of the Castle —the one which impresses us with its strength—is to be obtained from the kitchen-gardens. We see that the wall of the fortress formed a parallelogram, with fourteen towers varying in size. The old castle gardens or pleasance run down to the edge of the moat and at one corner stands a fine specimen of a dove-cote, in which pigeons and doves were reared by the hundred. The building from the outside has every appearance of being as warlike in character as its kindred towers, but a glance inside proves that it was erected for quite a peaceful and domestic object. Holes, bewildering in number, are let into the walls all round and inside each aperture is another one running at right angles, in which the birds could build their nests and rear their young out of sight and in security. There is a similar dove-cote at Westenhanger, known as " Fair Rosamond's Bower," but this one at Allington is larger.

Coming back to the outer bailey we go through the Tudor porch which has been built up against the Early English gateway which led to the old banquetting hall. Nothing but parts of the wall of the latter remain except the large fireplace, and flowers grow in sheltered beds on the spot which was once the floor, trodden by lordly gallant and bashful dame, keen archer and jovial halberdier, knightly lord and lowly retainer, where could be "heard the shout from wassail board, when knight and vassal pledged their lord." At one end is the entrance to the present house, and on the right of the door has recently been discovered a window of Early English character inside and of later date outside. Upon the masonry of the window and doorway are masons' marks. Talking of marks reminds us that Mr. Falcke has found several stones about the grounds chiselled with the initials of Henry Wyatt.

Inside the house everything has been done to maintain the original intentions of the architecture as far as possible. One of the towers has been tastefully brought into requisition for use as bedrooms— circular and old-fashioned in the extreme. One is supposed to be the chapel, as the window faces due east; there is a space for an altar, there is a niche at the side, and the doorway has a very peculiar "squint."

Tragedy, romance and comedy are strangely mixed up in the history of Allington Castle. All the three Wyatts were remarkable men, and it is perhaps for this reason that so much confusion exists. The other day, for instance, a portrait was pointed out to me in a gallery as the likeness of Sir Thomas Wyatt, "who was beheaded on Tower Hill and who was fed in his prison by a cat." A pretty muddle this. For it was Sir Henry Wyatt, the grandfather of Sir Thomas, the "Kentish rebel," whose feline friend saved him from starvation, and it was through him that the Allington property came into the possession of the Yorkshire family. Sir Henry took part in the rebellion against Richard the Third, was captured, imprisoned and tortured. According to a correspondent in the "Gentleman's Magazine" he was tortured by the barnacles and on this account a pair of barnacles is to be seen on the Wyatt arms. He was rewarded for his sufferings after the death of Richard by being knighted and receiving many honours at the King's hands. He greatly improved Allington Castle and during his residence the place was full of visitors and the old bailey must have been the scene of many a revel. The tradition about the cat is as follows. While he lay in the tower a cat one night crawled through the bars of his cell. The hapless prisoner and his four-footed visitor became fast friends and the legend states that the latter would every night go forth and capture a pigeon and bring it to her friend. It is unkind to enquire too closely into the truth of the story. Let it suffice to show why in the portraits of Sir Henry a cat is always represented and on a Wyatt monument in Boxley Church it is stated that he "ever made much of cats, as other men will of their spaniels or hounds." The Earl of Romney owns a painting in which Sir Henry is depicted sitting in his cell with a cat upon the window sill and a dead pigeon beside it. This, the first of the Wyatts who settled in Kent, was buried in the church at Milton-next-Gravesend.

A poet was Sir Thomas Wyatt, Sir Henry's son, and here at Allington many were the heartsick verses penned to Anne Boleyn, his lady-love. In young days they had met and plighted their troth, and as Wyatt was at Allington and Sir Thomas Boleyn at Hever Castle the two spent much time together. But alas for the faithful heart! Henry the Eighth was a frequent visitor to Boxley and Allington and here he saw the lovely Anne and determined to secure her for his own. Whether she was enamoured of her admirer's high estate and forsook Wyatt of her own accord, or whether she was impelled by her ambitious father to take the fatal step that brought her to her doom will never be known. The sequel was distressing enough. She suffered death on the scaffold, her body being surreptitiously carried from the Tower by her first lover and reverently buried, while he

became old before his time and died at the early age of thirty-
eight during a journey through Dorset.   His great consolation was
that his book of poems was the last read by Anne Boleyn before
her death.   From the scaffold she sent a jewel to him with the one
word, "Remember," Mary Wyatt, Sir Thomas' sister, being the mes-
senger. Leland calls him "incomparable;" Wood the historian describes
him as "the delight of the muses and mankind."   A plucky soldier, a
scholar and a courtier, Sir Thomas was never happier than when
wandering in the pleasance at Allington and the woods around, or
writing sonnets no doubt in one of the little circular tower rooms
that can still be seen.   Tennyson in "Queen Mary" makes the
younger Sir Thomas Wyatt speak thus of his father :—

> " Courtier of many courts he loved the more
> His own gray towers, plain life and lettered peace,
> To read and rhyme in solitary fields,
> The lark above, the nightingale below,
> And answer them in song."

Tragic and pathetic is the end of this poet-lover—his promised bride
torn from his side and wedded to another and cruelly done to death;
persecuted by his heartless monarch, loaded with honours and then
spitefully imprisoned more than once under some paltry pretext.
Judging from the strain of his sonnets one would think him weak.
But the assumption is wrong.   No braver man ever lived and many
were his doughty deeds as a soldier.   The story too is told of how
he once kept a lion whelp and a greyhound at Allington.   The
former grew until its youthful playfulness developed into mature
ferocity.   But still Wyatt allowed it freedom about the grounds.
One day, however, it sprang at his throat and his life was only
saved by the greyhound leaping upon the young lion and dragging
it to the ground.   Thereupon his master drew his sword and slew
the lion.   Henry the Eighth is said to have expressed astonishment
at Sir Thomas' coolness.   "Ah!" he exclaimed, "he's a brave man
who can tame lions."   It was this same Wyatt, too, who prompted
King Henry to carry on his crusade against the Roman Catholics.
One day the monarch was hard pressed by the Papists, felt unequal
to the task he had imposed upon himself, and appeared to be on the
point of surrendering.   "It is a hard thing, sire, that a King of England cannot repent without the Pope's leave," said Sir Thomas in a
chiding tone.   The monarch's pride was aroused, and he went forward with the Reformation with greater zest than before.

Henry the Eighth was a frequent visitor to Allington and a chair, which is supposed to have belonged to him, is now to be seen in Maidstone Museum. It was presented by the Earl of Romney and was found among old furniture at Allington. Its state of preservation is bad, but it bears traces of elaborate upholstery and the wood is inlaid with pearl. With the chair is connected a legend to the effect that any lady who sat in it should be kissed by King Henry and an inscription still to be seen on the chair bears out the story. The words are as follows:—

of thiss (chay)re iss entytled too one salute from everie ladie thott settes downe in itt.

Castell	y
Alynton	Hen 8
1530.	Rex.

The first words are missing, but they were probably "The owner" or something to that effect. That the Merry Monarch exacted toll from the fair ladies of Allington is a question about which very little doubt need be felt.

The third Wyatt who lived at Allington was the leader of the ill-fated Kentish rebellion. From youth upwards Sir Thomas had been a bold, harum-scarum, daring fellow and with little difficulty the rebels persuaded him to throw in his lot with them and lead them on to their fatal march to London. Historians are not unanimous in their estimate of his character. By some he is accused of being absurdly reckless, by others a deep schemer, by others a conscientious Protestant who dreaded a return to Popery if Mary married Philip, and by others a puppet in the hands of stronger men who pressed him forward and hid themselves behind the scenes. Anyway he paid for his action with his head, for Queen Mary never hesitated to have him executed when once he surrendered, riding ignominiously up the Strand seated on a horse behind his captor. Tennyson, who knew Allington well, and used to stay with a relative in the neighbourhood, lays the first scene of the second act of "Queen Mary" in the courtyard of the Castle. Here came the fifty leaders of the men who had collected at neighbouring Penenden Heath and besought Wyatt to lead them to London. At last he submitted. His farewell—his last farewell to his old home was this:—

"Ah, gray old Castle of Allington, greenfield
Beside the brimming Medway, it may chance
That I shall never look upon you more."

By the irony of fate Allington Castle was used as the prison of the insurgents captured by Sir Robert Southwell, sheriff of Kent. In his report to the Council Sir Robert stated that he committed "such as be of substance to Alyngton Castell," the others he sent to Maidstone gaol.

So much for the tragedy and romance that surround the old Castle. Let us now turn with a lighter heart to comedy. The story is this. During the time of Sir Henry Wyatt the abbot of neighbouring Boxley Abbey was a jovial gentleman whose fun and frolic frequently led him into difficulties. Allington Castle was a place he loved, because of the lavish hospitality of the host and hostess. Here he was treated to the best of fare, but one day he overstepped the rules of propriety by "making too free with the maid servants." Sir Henry was away from home—possibly a reason for his indiscretion. But he had Lady Wyatt to deal with. Upon discovering the abbot's misdeeds she raised neither uproar nor complaint but calmly gave orders that his holy legs should be placed in the stocks. Her commands were obeyed, and chafing under the jeers and laughter of passers-by the unworthy abbot spent several weary hours in the stocks just outside the castle gates. Instead of taking his punishment lightly the foolish fellow must needs appeal to the Privy Council, and this body called upon Sir Henry for an explanation of his wife's conduct. The owner of Allington turned the tables on the councillors by telling them that if they condemned his wife they would lie themselves open to the charge of condoning the abbot's offence and being fond of playing with maid-servants themselves. So the Privy Councillors wisely dropped the matter—evidence that morals, even among the abbots of the country, were pretty lax in those days.

A DOUBLE DORMER

KIT'S COTY HOUSE

THE CHEQUERS.

THE BRIDGE AND CHURCH

THE "COUNTLESS" STONES

THE OLD GEORGE.

AYLESFORD.

——

YLESFORD! Who has not heard of Aylesford? Pepys mentions it—"I light out of the way to see a Saxon monument, a thing of great antiquity"—Hasted waxes eloquent on its relics, every history of England contains its name. Through Aylesford came all those who wished to cross the Medway near this spot, for here the water ran shallow. Just outside Aylesford is the big slope over which ancient Briton Saxon fought in deadly conflict; where King Alfred drove the Danish Pirates pell-mell in their retreat to the Thames, where Edmond Ironside also pursued the Danes; where Druidical sacrifices were offered up; where Cavalier and Roundhead struggled in many a manly fight. Yes, here in the little village, lying snug in the valley of the Medway, we breathe the air of antiquity—not musty, mind you, for all that, but pure, bracing air that invigorates and imparts strength to carry you up and down the hillside in search of historic relics.

At Aylesford you can give play to your wildest imagination. There is nothing absolutely certain about many things—so much supposition. Mind you, we meet men who know. Why, I have talked on the subject of Kit's Coty House and other remains on the slopes of Blue Bell Hill with four different antiquaries and not two of them agree. Yet each one knows that his theory is absolutely correct. And again with legends and local traditions. I have had them related by different people and each good soul has his own version. So to be fair I have mentioned the lot in the course of my article and you, my readers, may take the one that is most acceptable to your palate.

Up in the fields most of these are to be found, but down below on the banks of the river many picturesque objects can be seen. There is the old fourteenth century bridge, a massive stone structure with its heavy piers which support the large arch in the centre and the two smaller ones on either side. This fine old bridge is doomed, not on account of decay—it would seemingly carry any weight—but because the wide piers take up so much space that when the water rushes down in time of flood the buttresses check it and send it helter skelter over the banks into the village street. The houses are in most instances protected by the erection of stone and brick walls, but in the lower part, near the George hostelry, the flood plays havoc in wet seasons. Sad that such a fine old structure should have to be sacrificed, and perhaps now, at the eleventh hour, some other way of meeting the difficulty caused by the flood can be discovered. For it is a magnificent old bridge. Many suggestions for its preservation have been made. Surely the simplest plan is to clear away the river banks in front of the outer arches. Two at least of these are rendered useless by the mass of earth in front of them. Were they opened up the water would have a much freer flow.

Looking at the bridge from the water's edge from the opposite side of the village we have a delightful view. Just across the stream lie barges, laden and unladen, with tan-coloured sails hanging over the sides ; in the lane which runs down to the water's edge prominently stands out the white and timbered front of a saddler's shop, throwing into shade the grey, old-fashioned, low-pitched hostelry known as the " George." Just above the bridge we get a glimpse of a row of gabled Queen Anne houses, renovated but in keeping with the old-world traditions of the place. Still higher rises the church, flanked on either side by graceful trees. The water at our feet flows and ebbs with the tide, and although in recent years fish life has become rare so far down the river old anglers will tell you strange tales. Mind you, they are fishermen's yarns ! Believe them if you like. One states that at dead of night a fearful commotion was heard down by the river. Torches were brought and under their glare could be seen a fox thrusting his legs deep into the soft mud, while in the water wriggled a huge pike, having in its capacious thousand-toothed jaws half the fox's head and struggling to appease its appetite with the body. The tug of war was ended when some men crushed in the head of the pike and captured both fish and its victim. The story you will say requires a lot of swallowing, more perhaps than the fox,

Another story which shows the cunning of the pike tells us that a big forty-pounder—these big fish are always forty-pounders—was wont to prowl about under Aylesford Bridge. Time after time anglers got him on their tackle with sparkling dace, soft-fleshed gudgeon or glistening spoon. But it was always the same story. Immediately the old gentleman found himself hooked he swam round and round one of the piers of the bridge, tightened the line, shook his head and snapped the tackle. The end of this fish I know not. He may still be playing his same old trick under another bridge on the Medway.

Let us now stroll along the village street, which does not impress one with great beauty. Two old hostelries stand out prominently however. In the higher part of the road is the "Chequers," a long low-pitched building said to be at least 400 years old. Its wooden courses are supported by massive brackets, while its dormer windows and the two bays have carved work beneath them. Remarkable little windows close up under the eaves complete the picture. If you go inside the quaint old building—which, by-the-bye, is about to be repaired but not altered in character—you will see on the floor of the kitchen some unique brick-work of herring-bone pattern. The other old hostelry is the "George," standing near the bridge. Seventeen years ago the building was thoroughly renovated and much of its ancient appearance altered. There is a date of 1774 on the front, but this can only denote the year in which some restorations were made, for the structure itself dates back to a much earlier period. When the front was repaired an old carved doorway was discovered but blocked up again with cement. Strangely enough, one part of the smoking room is in Aylesford and the other in Rochester parish. Walking further down the street the other old building which attracts your attention is one with a double dormer—two windows for two separate storeys—but its efforts to stand upright have failed with years and at the present time it is tumbling backwards into the slanting roof of the house.

We now mount the zig-zag hill which leads to the church, for high above the level, even higher than the housetops, stands the churchyard enclosed by a wall. The body of the church looks small and out of proportion to the fine square tower, which, by-the-bye, is said to have been built long before the rest of the edifice and was used for defensive purposes—to cover the river below. Some authorities go to the extent of identifying it with the "Castellum"

quoted in Domesday, and arguing that it was built to guard the
Medway while the Saxon wooden church stood by its side. This
tower is of three stages with embattled parapet, and round the
courses are remarkable 15th century gurgoyles, and the upper stage
is of much later date than the lower portion. Glancing at the
south side of the church we find that everything looks modern, but
upon strolling in the opposite direction very old walls and the remains of older windows can be discerned.

Entering the church we pass through a pretty little modern porch
with the image of St. Peter over the outer doorway. The sun
peeping through the windows diffuses a variety of warm tints, for
this is one of the few churches which possesses only stained glass
windows. None of them are of great age, but some of more recent
date bear evidence of the improved colouring which of late years
has characterised this sort of work. On the whole, however, the
interior is gloomy.

One of its curiosities is a set of chimes worked by hand on the
ground floor. Any tune within a certain compass in the key of F
can be played, the ringer manipulating the bells by means of
tightened ropes. Each Sunday morning before service and again
before evensong a tune is rung by the sexton. The tower was
restored in 1878 through the generosity of Mr. H. A. Brassey, of
Preston Hall, and he it was who presented the chimes in 1885.
Up in the belfry can be seen an old square of lead taken from
the roof of the tower when it was repaired. The date is 1687,
and the names inscribed on it are P. Palmer and T. Pack, who
were churchwardens when the roof was restored in 1687. Until
about thirty years ago the sanctus bell was rung. In the old days
this bell was rung at the elevation of the Host, but at Aylesford,
now Protestant, it was tolled at the close of morning service.
This same sanctus bell is now at St. Mark's Church, Eccles.

The remains of the simple Norman church of Aylesford are to
be seen in the nave and choir. From the former a large aisle is
separated by five arches. It will be noticed that the arcades in
the chancel are evidently of later Perpendicular style than those in
the nave. The last arch from the nave is broken, and one theory
which explains this peculiarity is that while the arcades were being
pulled down the workmen were suddenly stopped in their vandalism.
In the chancel, however, are the gems of the church. The vestry
is curtained off from the chancel and here is a huge monument

erected to the memory of Sir John Banks, who died in 1699. The figures, if anything, are larger than life-size, being clad in ancient Roman costumes. The armour-clad bodies and Stuart wigs make a remarkable mixture. Just below this monument is a brass, dated 1426, placed there to the memory of John Cossington and his wife Sarra. The male figure is clad in plate armour, while beneath his feet is a lion. Part of the inscription, asking for prayers for the repose of his soul, has been at some time partially erased, it is assumed by the Puritans. Fixed in the vestry is a small palimpsest brass—a brass engraved on both sides. In this case the original one was cut in two, part of a female figure being seen at the back, and it was evidently part of a large Flemish brass. On the front is an inscription recording the death of Henry Savell, servant to Sir Thomas Wyatt. The date is 1545, but the engraving suggests a much earlier time. There is a fine oak screen that now divides the vestry from the chancel aisle. It used to divide the aisle from the chancel, no doubt taking the place of the unsuitable iron railings now in use.

As an altar tomb stands a magnificent monument to the Colepeppers in the form of a male and female figure with smaller ones representing the children of the union. It is beautifully carved and relieved by rich colouring, which has been preserved by modern restoration. The inscription is as follows:—" Here lyeth intombed Sir Thomas Colepepper, Knight by bloode and descente, descended of many worthye ancestors; in his lifetime for his worth and desarte beloved of all men, and in his death a much lamented and bemoned; he had by Dame Marie his only wife, at the time of his decease three sonnes and two daughters, which Dame Marie to perform her last duty in remembrance of her faithfvll love to her deceased husband at her own cost erected the gratefvll monvment vnder which he resteth, and by his lively faith hopeth in a joyfvll resvrection; he dyed 12 Oct., 1604." Hanging on the walls of the chancel is some old funeral armour. It was placed for a short time in Maidstone Museum, but very properly brought back again to Aylesford and placed in its original position in the church walls. In the north chancel is buried Lady Taylor, of Preston Hall. Her history was a remarkable one. She was the daughter of Sir Richard Colepepper, of Preston Hall, who died in 1659, and had four husbands —Herbert Stapeley, of Patcham, Sussex, and M.P. for Seaford; Sir Thomas Taylor, Bart., of Park House, Maidstone, who left a son to succeed to the baronetcy; her cousin, Thomas Colepepper, of Hollingbourne, a barrister; and Doctor John Milner, of Pudsey, Yorkshire. All four died, while she outlived her children and died at Preston Hall, lonely but beloved by the poor in 1734 at the age of 80. It was from her father that she inherited Preston Hall and finally settled it upon her fourth husband. He, however, died young, and the estates went to his brother Charles, who was also a physician and died in 1771.

It should be added that Sir Paul Rycant, the Oriental traveller and author, was buried in Aylesford church. In the tower there is a tablet erected to the memory of one Rosamond Spong, a "left-handed" descendant of Charles II., who died in 1840, aged 92 years. She lived at Mill Hall. Near here, in the north-east pillar of the tower, is a long square opening from which you can obtain a glimpse of a part of the north wall of the church. This is presumed to be a leper squint, and it is further urged that at one time there was a communion table in that part of the church which is visible from the hole.

The church plate consists of a cup with paten cover with the date letter of 1627, a flagon of 1711, a larger paten of 1724 and three alms dishes dated 1724 and 1858, one of the latter being given by Lady Alicia Taylor.

A glance through the parish register well repays the trouble of deciphering some of the old handwriting. Unfortunately, some six or seven years ago, during the time that Canon Grant was the incumbent of the living, the oldest register was lost. Together with some of the communion plate it was taken to Rochester to be placed on exhibition, but never returned. Whether it was lost on the road or stolen cannot be said; if the latter, one wonders what special attraction the old book can have to cause anybody to run the risk of criminal proceedings. And yet, perchance, a pretty romance or startling scandal is woven round an entry therein upon which the happiness of more than one person depends.

Two of the old volumes of the register still remain, however, extending over a period of 177 years, from 1635 to 1812. On the fly-leaf of the later one we find it recorded that in the year 1811 the population of the parish was as follows:—157 houses, 175 families, two houses building, one house uninhabited; 114 families employed in agriculture, 56 in trade, six not comprised in either; 341 males, 534 females; total 875. Amongst the births we find an

entry to the effect that "Thomas, son of Mr. Robert and Elizabeth Pleydell was baptised December 30th, 1737." This is apparently the only case in the whole register in which the title "Mr."
is used. At one period the grammar of the sexton who made the
entries was evidently at fault, for we find more than one entry
similar to the following :—"Sarah, daughter of Abraham, and Anne
Clark were baptised June 10th, 1739." In every year there appeared
to be a large number of children belonging to "travellers" baptised
at Aylesford, this place being, before the railway came into existence,
of much greater importance than at present. One of the most curious
entries is the following :—"Thomas Rawling Mallock, son of ————
was born ———— and bap^{td} 21st Sept., 1766." The parents of the
child and the date of its birth are both left blank, for what reason
it is difficult to surmise. Some strange Christian names are to be
seen. One poor child lived for ten days only under the name of
Chatharina Francess Philadelphia Lake. Kitural was the name be-
stowed upon a poor unoffending girl whose parents had been given
the homely names of John and Elizabeth. One would judge that
some confusion would be caused as the result of the following
entries :—"John, son of John and Mary Tunbridge, was baptised
January 8th, 1743." "John, son of Edmund and Mary Tunbridge,
was baptised March 18th, 1743." In the registry of burials we find
some very quaint entries :—"A woman being delivered of a female
child, some supposed her to be the wife of one William Man : others
saide her name was . . . . Jarrett: both she and her childe died
and were buried the vvth day of Sept., 1656." In 1665 "a travelling
man who sold earthen pots and other earthen ware being found dead
in Thomas Smith's barn was buried in the said Thomas Smith's
orchard the said seventh day of November." A few years ago some
remains were found in Cossington Orchard, and they are supposed
to be the relics of this man of earthenware. Apparently Londoners
have always visited Kent for the hop-picking season for "Thomas
Hillery (a child aged about 21 months), the sone of John Hillery
and of Elizabeth his wife, whose dwelling place (as they say) is in
Whit-Chappel : and travelling for harvest and hopping work, lodged
at the Sign of the Blew Bell in this parish, when the said sone,
Thomas Hillery died, and was buried here at Aylesford the vvj^{th} day
of August, 1670." It should be remembered that a hundred years
ago Aylesford was famous for its many hop gardens ; now there is
not a hop grower in the parish. As in all other registers mention

is made of woollen burials. The bitterness that existed between religious sects can be gathered from the following :—" Anne, the daughter of John Dawson and of Mary, his wife, was born on the 25th day of August, 1709, but was never baptised by reason they profess themselves to be of that eronious sect of the Dippers or Anabaptists." Tragedy is chronicled by the following :—" Mary Willard was buried February 20th, 1758. Mary Willard hanged herself and was deemed by the coroner and his inquest distracted." A remarkable occurrence in the register is the entries in connection with the Vintons. Robert and Anne Vinton had children in 1699, 1705, 1708, 1714. In 1716 Elizabeth, one of their children, died and the same year another daughter was born and named after the deceased child. Shortly after the birth of the latter Anne Vinton died. Every entry in connection with the Vintons is written in a large black handwriting, apparently done to especially mark the occurrences. Yet I can find no trace of any Vintons being people of note in the village.

In the churchyard are many interesting things. Just at the foot of the east wall are to be seen three stone coffin lids that were taken up from the floor of the church and placed in their present position. They are in a good state of preservation considering the exposed position—a pity they were brought into the open air, for the carving is well done. The most southerly of these stones has been copied for a modern gravestone, with the additional decoration of a chalice and bible. It is over the grave of Archdeacon Grant and his wife, who lie buried in the north-west of the graveyard. Archdeacon Grant was a former vicar of the parish. Close to the tomb of Archdeacon Grant is the memorial to Mr. H. A. Brassey. It takes an allegorical form, there being a figure of a woman being consoled by an angel. The features are very delicately chiselled and the expression on the faces of the two figures is simply life-like. The one looks the very image of abject misery and despair, the other is radiant with hope and sympathy. Near the porch is the plain, solid marble monument that marks the burial place of Mr. E. L. Betts. As you enter the churchyard, and nearly opposite the porch, a large tombstone stands to your right. It is a memorial to one John Spong. He is supposed to have been the original of Dickens' "Wardle" in the "Pickwick Papers." A country house called Cobb Tree, about a mile from Aylesford, was introduced by the great novelist as "Dingley Dell," where the hospitable Mr. Wardle lived and entertained the immortal Pickwick. The gem of the churchyard lies back almost out of sight. It is moss-eaten, but the inscription remains plainly visible. Erected in 1715 to one Richard Austen, it runs as follows :—

EPITAPH ON A BLACKSMITH.

My Sledge and Hammer lyes declyned,
My Bellows too have lost their wind,
My Fire's extinct, My Forge decaid,
And in the dust my Vice is laid;
My Coal is spent, my Irons gone,
My Nails are drove, my work is done.

Near the east wall is a tombstone standing on legs in the form of a table. It takes one back to the tombs of the Chinese, whose idea is to leave the sides open and allow the spirit to escape if it wishes.

Coming away from the church we are reminded that up till within thirty years ago the lock-up cage used to be in the high church wall on the hill leading out of the village towards the Friars. It was built into the wall and fronted by bars of iron. The parish pound which stood at the top of this same hill is now hardly recognisable as the tool house of the Parish Council, with its corrugated iron roof. The transformation was effected five years ago. The mortuary stands adjoining the churchyard on the opposite side of the road to the pound. It was built three or four years ago by the Parish Council.

One of the most excellent institutions in Aylesford is the Hospital of the Holy Trinity, or, as the rooms are now called, the Almshouses. They consist of fourteen rooms built of grey stone and catch the eye of the passer-by along the Chatham road, standing as they do high on a bank on the left-hand side. The Hospital was built in 1605 by Sir William Sedley from money left by his brother, John Sedley, "for six poor aged and impotent persons in the Street, always provided that one of the six shall be able to read prayers morning and evening." For the purpose of maintaining the charity, Sir William invested further money in the purchase of Bubhurst Farm in Frittenden. After a time it lapsed and the charity was entirely lost sight of, the building being in a very dilapidated state, but used as a farmhouse. Whilst rummaging amongst the old ruins the wife of the occupier found some old documents which she handed over to a Mr. Thomas Robson, a lawyer who lived at the Cedars. Acting upon these Mr. Robson at his own expense fought a long lawsuit with the holders of the property belonging to the charity, and after some time, in 1842 to be precise, the houses were restored and the money vested in trustees to prevent it again lapsing. In 1892 four more rooms were added, erected by his widow and children to the memory of Mr. H. A. Brassey, while the present owner of Preston Hall, Mr. H. L. C. Brassey, son of the gentleman to the memory of whom the houses were erected, has endowed it with £100 a year. In addition to the Sedley and Brassey Charities the Savidge and Faunce Charities have been merged into the Hospital. In 1625 Patrick Savidge bequeathed " £60 a year for a continual stock for the use of the poor people of Aylesford," while in 1713 Sir Robert Faunce left a yearly sum of 10s. to be distributed on the feast of St. Swithin in money or bread by the church-wardens and overseers of the parish. At the back of the hospital, leading into the gardens from Mount Pleasant, is what was once a finely carved stone doorway. But the elements have played sad havoc with the stone and most of the inscription is gone. It is supposed to have come from the old chapel at the Friars. In the arch are inscribed words now illegible, while in the spandrels can be seen battered heads. A doorway, a copy of the one here, was made and now forms the entrance to the chancel from the south side of the church, but of necessity the sculptor was compelled to fall back upon his own imagination in producing the figures and inscriptions.

The Wesleyan Church stands on the right-hand side of the Chatham road and was built about fifty years ago. The exact date of the erection is not known, as the old books in connection with the building have by some means or other been lost. Thirty years ago it was enlarged. Before the erection of the present chapel the Methodists, it is said, used to meet over a stable in the centre of the village. Others say that the services were held over a wheelwright's shop in the centre of the village, the place now being occupied by a bootmaker.

As we saunter along the road to Maidstone and Boxley we notice on our left-hand side two excellent recreation grounds. The larger one and the one nearer the village is the ground that belongs to the Aylesford Athletic Club and is rented by them from

Mr. H. L. C. Brassey. Mr. Brassey in 1897 kindly erected a pavilion on the ground and gave it to the club as a memorial of the late Queen Victoria's Diamond Jubilee. The smaller ground beyond the Athletic Ground belongs to the Parish Council and is devoted entirely to the recreation of children.

We have so far been spending our time on one side of the river. But on the other where the railway station stands is a very trim well-groomed road and many trim well-groomed buildings. Here stands the Infants' School, erected and presented to the village by Mr. E. L. Betts, and to commemorate this event the inhabitants erected a fountain in the playground. Mr. Betts was also the means of securing a pure water supply for the village. Built by the school is the Institute, which the same gentleman renovated in 1865. Mr. Brassey still allows the villagers the room rent free, while a caretaker is also provided. Among other benefits conferred upon Aylesford by Mr. Betts were the pottery and brick-making works, which give employment to a great number of men.

Preston Hall, lately the seat of Mr. Henry Leonard Campbell Brassey, lies on the south side of the river in a finely wooded park of about two hundred acres. It is quite a modern house, having been only built in 1857 by the late Mr. E. L. Betts. The date of building is on the weather vane. The site of the old mansion was just below where the present one stands, part of the actual site being covered by an aviary. The old prints of the place show a plain, white, ugly, square building, apparently of the Elizabethan age, standing below the eminence on which the present building stands, and somewhat nearer the village. There is still an old barn near the house on the window frame of which are the letters T.C. The present house is now creeper clad, and as we glide past in the train it arouses our admiration. The main entrance is from the Maidstone to London road and the drive leads in a direct line to the handsome porch, added to the building twenty years ago. From the porch, looking towards the gates, which are of hand wrought iron work, and have only lately been erected by Mr. Brassey, can be seen "the green drive" stretching away into the distance till it becomes but a narrow belt of grass, fringed with the darker hues of the trees. The entrance hall is an imposing piece of ornamentation, the principal attraction being three fine pieces of tapestry. The one on the right represents the marching of the Saxons to the battle of Aylesford, the centre piece (the largest of the three) represents the death of Horsa at the battle. Horsa is lying supported by his comrades, while in the middle distance are servants holding the terrified steed of the fallen warrior. On the left is a representation of the burning of Rochester Bridge. On the opposite side of the house to the porch is the dining-room with its richly panelled oak walls decorated with armour and swords. The ceiling is very lofty and richly decorated in colours. The drawing-room opens from the morning-room by a sliding glass door, and thence one catches the glimpse of a very fine conservatory. There is a large amount of oak carving—practically modern, of course, but none the less beautiful—about the house, especially on the door of the library, where the monogram E.L.B. can be traced. A splendid view of the park can be obtained from the tower. Straight away to the south stretches the main drive and the green drive divided by the narrow white stretch of main road and the beautiful iron-work gates. Then all around on either side one sees the verdant surface of the park dotted here and there with graceful deer, now peacefully grazing, then flying off with agile feet. To the north-east we catch just a glimpse of the stud farm, while on the south-west, shimmering through the trees, we see the artificial lake. By the way, a story is attached to this lake. It is said that after it had been made some few years the water and fish entirely disappeared through the bottom. This is true certainly, but the explanation does away with the mystery that seems to envelop the incident according to some of the villagers. The clay bottom gave way and naturally the water oozed away through the subsoil. Mention has been made above of the stud farm. Mr. Brassey was a well-known breeder of race-horses, and it was a common sight round Preston Hall to see beautiful animals enclosed in a specially fenced field. Mr. Brassey recently sold Preston Hall to Mr. Robert Horner, and the residence is at present unoccupied.

It should be added that old Preston Hall was the home of a branch of the famous Kentish family of Colepeppers, and it is con-tended that the letters T.C. on the barn are the initials of one of the Thomas Colepeppers. To give any idea of the services rendered to the county by this family would fill volumes, for we find them scattered all over Mid Kent and one can scarcely enter a church in the vicinity of Maidstone without finding a monument or tablet erected to members of it. As Hasted rightly says, this family " produced men who became eminent as warriors and statesmen in the different ages in which they lived."

Quite away to the north-west, one-and-a-half miles distant from Aylesford, is the old manor of Eccles, now no longer a manor house with lands around it, but a populous district and a village in itself with a population of 1,000 inhabitants. It has sprung up within the last fifty years, and has grown with the increasing prosperity of the Burham cement works. Thirty years ago there were only fifty houses in the place, but now there are streets of modern cottages, a modern church, a modern institute and a modern air about the place that is indisputable. The actual site of the old manor house is unknown, but some people are inclined to think that Rowe Place, so called from a famous family, a low-lying house with a long frontage, situated on the left of the road from Aylesford to Eccles, is the place. As, however, the manor was sufficiently old to have been in the possession of Odo Bishop of Bayeaux in the reign of William the Conqueror this is extremely doubtful. Near Eccles are the remains of a Roman town, and large quantities of ancient titles have been found there.

Having exhausted the sights in the village and adjacent spots down by the river let us now stroll up the slope towards Blue Bell Hill. The latter is the main road between Maidstone and Rochester and from its summit the grandest view of the fertile Medway valley can be obtained. To reach the hill we stroll out of the village by the road which reminds one of Hollingbourne, for, like that neighbouring village, it has a stream running down the side. This water comes from the old fish ponds which we shall visit presently.

We pass on our left a huge sand and gravel pit—an enormous one covering several acres—and here a great number of fossils and remains of animals have been dug up. They are now in the Maidstone Museum and include among other things immense tusks, once nine feet long but now crumbling into small pieces, bones of the great elk, the backbone of a rhinoceros, a lion's skull, and parts of other beasts now extinct in England in the wild state. In 1898 a human skeleton was found, the body having apparently been buried in a contracted position. By the side of the bones was found a bronze flat celt eight inches long and two bronze knife-daggers, the rivets of which, used for fastening them to the handle, were in excellent preservation. Upon being exposed to the air the bones crumbled to dust and now only an arm-bone remains. Archæologists place the date of the bones as being 1500 to 2000 years before Christ. There are to be seen burials of three different periods, the most interesting find being a late Celtic urn-field. Most of the relics found there are in the museum at Oxford.

Passing along the road which takes us in a direct line to Kit's Coty ouse, the outline of which cuts the horizon, we pause before a cluster of trees in a field on our right. Here lie the stones which have gone by the name of the Countless Stones from time immemorial. The stones no doubt originally formed one of the cremlecks, monuments erected in England before the introduction of Christianity, and it is said that this special pile was wrecked by the growth of an elm tree. The decayed trunk of this old elm can still be seen clinging to a huge slab, but from its healthier roots have sprung three young trees. The stones, of all shapes and sizes, lie in confusion and half hidden in the ground and brushwood. It is said that nobody can count them correctly, and I must confess that upon visiting the place with three friends the other day, each of us counted the stones and brought out a different total—anything between seventeen and twenty-one. A ghastly story is told about these stones. Many, many years ago a certain baker of Aylesford determined to arrive at a correct solution, so he appeared on the scene with a basket full of tiny loaves. Round the pile he went carefully placing a loaf on each stone. So far so good. Next he proceeded to count the loaves and place them in his basket. One, two, three he picked up and so on, until he reached the last. In a voice of triumph he stooped forward and was about to call aloud the fatal number when with a gasp he fell dead! There is a variation in the story by which the baker, upon counting the stones afterwards, found one more loaf than he brought with him—a weird freak ascribed to the Evil One.

Returning to the road we follow it till the sign post is reached. From this point the road branches off—on the right to Maidstone and on the left to Rochester. This is not Blue Bell Hill, that is higher—but none other than the Pilgrims' Way. Like other parts of this historic road it lies under the lea of a hill.

Pressing forward up a narrow lane and through an arable field we reach the world-famed Kit's Coty House. This consists of four large stones, the immense one which forms the roof being a slab about ten tons in weight and twelve feet in length ; the two side stones run about eight and seven feet respectively. There are various theories about the origin of this old monument, one that it marks the spot where Catigern was slain and buried, the other that it is of more ancient date and was an altar erected by the Ancient Britons and used by the Druids for human sacrifice. Then again some argue that this spot was once the site of a huge cemetery— the various heaps of stones in the vicinity extending over to Addington bearing out this view—and that it was an altar from which the priests offered up prayers for the repose of the souls of the dead around them. But the most plausible theory makes it the sepulchral chamber of a barrow, once entirely covered by earth, and that, by stress of heavy rains and from its position on a slope of the hill, the soil above it was by degrees swept away, leaving it open to view as at present. As Neolithic stone implements have been found near here it is argued that this barrow was made earlier than the Bronze age—about 1500 years B.C.

There seems but little doubt that the great battle, in which the Britons under Vortimer defeated the Saxons under Hengest, Catigern, the brother of Vortimer, was slain, and, so it is alleged, buried under Kit's Coty House, while the Saxons lost Horsa who was buried at Horsted near Rochester. It will be remembered that the Britons soon discovered their mistake in seeking the assistance of the Saxons and, finding their erstwhile friends turned into foes, were compelled to fight for their very lives. Here at Aylesford the two armies met. What a sight it must have been! No smoke from gunpowder, every foe clearly outlined for attack. No distant firing, the whole conflict one deadly embrace, knee to knee, breast to breast, separated only by the length of a heavy club or flint-pointed spear. And giants all of them, men of herculean strength. Why, we read that Horsa was killed by Vortimer, son of the Saxon leader, who, being closely pressed, tore up a young tree by the roots and with it dashed out the brains of his foe. Yes, truly 'twas a mighty battle. The result of the sanguinary fight is an open question among historians. Some state that the Saxons were victorious and followed up their advantage. Yet we are told that they returned to the Isle of Thanet and awaited reinforcements. Anyway we know that the Saxons finally overpowered the Britons, one great battle being fought at Crayford. The number of men on both sides killed at the battle under Blue Bell Hill was vast, and it is argued that the stones found all about the vicinity of Kit's Coty House marked the graves of the slain.

Besides the great fight between the Britons and Saxons it must be remembered that it was at Aylesford that the Danes escaped from the clutch of the Saxons after they had suffered defeat at Otford at the hands of Edmond Ironside. The escape occurred through the treachery of the Duke of Mercia, that Saxon chieftain, through jealousy of Edmond, withdrawing his forces and allowing the enemy, under Canute, to escape to the sea. Here also came the Danish pirates over a century earlier. King Alfred played havoc with the invaders at Fernham and chased them over the river at Aylesford, and so fiercely did he follow up his victory that according to Lambarde " they were compelled to take the Thaimse without boate or bridge, in which passage there were a great number of them drowned, the residue having ynough to doe to save their owne lives and convey over their captaine, that had received a deadly wound."

But to return to Kit's Coty House. Its name does not help to clear up the mystery. Philipott in 1659 says it meant a sheepcot; Drose in his "Antiquities" argues that "Kit" was an abbreviation of Catigern and "Coty" is really "coit," a large flat stone, and the whole means "Catigern's house built with coits." Then again I have heard it argued that the words should read Ked Coit, this being Celtic for "the tomb in the wood."

Along the side of the hill are old entrenchments dating back to the days of the Romans, and among the historic relics that have recently disappeared is a huge stone which was pointed out as the natural throne of Hengist when proclaimed first King of Kent.

But we have not finished our rambles on the slope of Blue Bell Hill. At the north side of the field which contains Kit's Coty House is a deep hole which has only recently been discovered and is known to but very few people. Under an elm tree is it situated and mixed up with the roots are many stones of various sizes, although smaller than characterise the neighbouring cremlecks. Deep down through these stones can be discerned a dark circular cavity. Just below the surface of the land lie the stones, but under them is the well-shaped hole. It appears to be about two feet in diameter and neatly built of stone the size of a brick. It has every appearance of a well. But why a well in this spot? There is no building near at the present day. One suggestion is that the Pilgrims on their way to Canterbury used it. But who would build it? Not they. For I sent down a stone attached to a piece of string and plumbed a depth of 112 feet. Is it likely they would burrow so deep? On the other hand one theory connects it with a subterranean passage, for local tradition concludes that the whole country hereabouts is undermined with them. As a matter of fact this hole lies in a direct line between Kit's Coty House and Kewland, and not only is it believed that subterranean passages lead from the former site in a cellar, but at Kewland an old entrance to an underground passage has been sealed up. Can this hole be connected with this passage? Is it a ventilating shaft? As a matter of fact I am rather dubious about subterranean passages. We hear of so many and see so few. Another suggested solution of the mystery points to the hole being the same as the well-like tombs of the East. If we lowered ourselves down this cavity, away below at a depth of over a hundred feet we should probably reach a great square chamber, a veritable chamber of death, with the remains of Celtic chieftains lying around—maybe nought but dust. Ghastly thought! But I have reserved the most probable theory till the end—that the hole is a well connected with one of the Roman villas which were known to stand here-about. By-the-bye, Kewland is a remarkable-looking old farmhouse with a peculiar stack of chimneys. Inside the building is a large wooden wheel turned by a dog for drawing water from the well, one of the few left in England.

In a field just below the Pilgrim's Way and almost in a line between Kit's Coty House and the village is a huge slab called the Coffin Stone owing to its peculiar shape. Still walking in the direction of the village we come to Tottington where the reservoirs for the water supply can be seen. Down from here runs the clearest of streams, linking together several pools known as the Fishponds. It is supposed that the White Friars used to catch their fish here. But in those days the water ran deeper, and it is easy to imagine that fine sport among the trout was obtained. The same stream runs along till it reaches the village and ripples down the side of the road which we mounted on our way to Kit's Coty House and the other grand old relics of a by-gone age that decks the slopes of Blue Bell Hill. Unsolved mysteries many of them. And therein lies their charm.

OLD CARMELITE PRIORY AT AYLESFORD.

———

ON the banks of the river Medway and close to the old part of the village of Aylesford stands one of the greatest treasures of monastic England. It is now called the Friars and is a private residence. Richard Lord de Grey was the founder in 1240, bringing over to England some Carmelites from Europe as he returned from the Crusades. The same nobleman subsequently founded another Carmelite Priory in London. And this fact clears up all doubt as to whether the Priory at Aylesford was the first one of its kind to exist in England. Lord de Grey married Isolda, daughter and co-heir of Hugh Bardolph, Lord of Hoo, from whom he inherited the land upon which the Priory was built, and according to Philipott many of his posterity were buried in the church of the Priory. It is of interest to know that the Carmelite house at Alnwick was founded at the same time by Lord de Vesey, a brother in arms of Lord de Grey. The Carmelites, or White Friars as they are more popularly known, were no doubt descended from the hermits of Mount Carmel, but one legend states that the prophet Elijah founded the Order, while a second legend goes to the extent of making the Virgin Mary a Carmelite nun.

Driven before the sword of the Saracens the White Friars aimlessly wandered about Europe, and it was no doubt one of these straggling bands that De Grey took compassion upon and brought to England. They were very strict in their observances and always walked bare-foot. Here at Aylesford they settled down in the Priory built in Aylesford Wood—for at this spot was a forest—and this Priory at Aylesford was an exact imitation of that

AN OLD MEDALLION

IN THE COURTYARD

THE FRIARS FROM THE GARDEN

AN OLD CORNER

THE ENTRANCE GATE

at Mount Carmel, where the founder had been an eye witness of the holy and austere living of these mendicants in the Wilderness of Palestine. The houses of this Order increased so rapidly in all parts of Christendom that in 1245 a general chapter was assembled at Aylesford. Simon Stock was chosen Superior-General of the Society. This Simon Stock lived in a hollow tree, and it was through his agency that the Order deteriorated into a mendicant one. He was afterwards canonised and buried at Bordeaux, where the Cathedral contains his relics and shrine. The White Friars from earnest religious men became tainted with the vices of kindred societies and in the end were suppressed. This was in the year 1538, Bishop Ingworth, suffragan Bishop of Dover, undertaking the work. Reporting upon the subject in that year he writes: "I have receyueyed the howse of whyte fryers in Aylesforde into the kyngs hands." After its suppression the Priory was given by Henry the Eighth to Sir Thomas Wyatt, whose son, the leader of the great Wyatt rebellion, forfeited it to the Crown when convicted of high treason, and Queen Elizabeth during her reign gave it to John Sedley. At the latter's death the property came into possession of his brother, Sir William Sedley, and he converted the old Priory into a residence, and it is said that during his lifetime "true objects of distress were always sure to find relief" at the Friars. The property next passed by sale to Sir Peter Ricaut, whose heir subsequently sold it to Caleb Banks, of Maidstone. The latter's son, Sir John Banks, baronet, did much to improve the mansion, and at his death the estate passed by marriage into the hands of the Heneages, one of whom became Earl of Aylesford. It has been in the possession of this family ever since, and the present Lady Aylesford at one time resided in the house. The tenant is now Mrs. Hunter. So much for the history of the old Priory, admittedly one of the best preserved of any in England. Recent tenants have treated it with careful hands, regardful of its historic value and determined to maintain its ancient appearance as much as possible.

We enter the historic and once sacred grounds through the original gateway, a square building more ancient than the Tudor arches which can be seen under the remains of some older ones. On the east side, cut out of large blocks of stone, are spy-holes, cross-shaped, from which the gate-keeper could watch the approach of strangers. And there were many such. The beggars, whose profession it was to roam the country and live on charity, never came to those old

priories in vain; but, in addition, weary pilgrims to and from Canterbury would turn off from Blue Bell Hill, walk through the
Aylesford Woods and seek shelter and food at the hands of the
friars. In the spandrels of an old doorway which leads into the
tower is the date 1590 on the right and a stag's head on the left.
The winding stairs lead you up to the top of the tower, from whence
a fine view can be obtained.

But perhaps the best view is the one we take from a corner
of the garden—a terrace now used as a bowling green, but still
called the Monks' Walk. It is here that the spirit of an imprisoned
monk is said to have appeared years after he was bricked up in an
old buttress. On a certain night in each year—so the story goes—
you could see his figure, wrapped in the white gown of the Carmelites, slowly strolling along the terrace, head downcast and himself
buried in thought. Suddenly there creeps from behind a tree two
friars, who, springing forward, catch their victim unawares, gag and
carry him towards the priory. No sound, but the stifled sob of a
half-suffocated man. Then all disappears. It is a pretty ghost story
and one I read about in an old volume. But the identical date of
this anniversary is not given—an omission of which most retailers
of ghost stories are guilty. Another blood-curdling tradition is, no
doubt, part and parcel of the one I have just related. Indeed, it
may be termed the last act of the tragedy. In the present drawing-
room of the house is a small chamber cut in the centre of a large
brick buttress. It may have been a priest's cell, but tradition asserts
that it was a secret dungeon wherein prisoners were done to death.
In early days the Carmelites were a holy and religious community,
but latterly they drifted into vicious ways that deservedly brought
disaster about their ears. And amid it all they made enemies.
These enemies sometimes mysteriously disappeared. Never again
were they seen. Who knows but that this secret chamber could
solve many a horrid mystery. What more easy to hide a crime in
it and finally sink the trace of guilt in the waters of the Medway
near by? But in this instance, it is said, one monk had offended
his brethren in a manner that no ordinary death could expiate. Into the chamber—this old cell in the buttress—was he thrust; food
and water sufficient to last him a few days were placed at his side,
and then—the wall was bricked up. What a death! Slow, but
sure. Such is the story that I am enabled to weave together from
a tangled skein. Many years ago the wall was pulled down and

there lay the skeleton of the monk. Maybe he is the one whose spirit walked along the terrace at night, and whose capture was wont to be re-enacted on a certain night in the year. As the skeleton, however, was given a decent burial after its discovery, the poor spirit is probably now at rest. At least that may explain why no one ever sees him now-a-days. Against the wall of the room and just outside the alcove hangs a plaster medallion of a monk's head. This is said to be a portrait of the wretched being who was incarcerated in the cell—as he appeared before his starvation surely, if one can judge from the plump cheeks and genial expression of the face.

As you enter the precincts of the Friars through the gateway it is at once apparent that great changes must have been made, and on this side of the monastery much of the ancient fabric was demolished by Sir John Banks. The trim lawns and gravel paths cover the foundations of many walls which Colonel T. B. Shaw-Hellier discovered by means of excavation during his residence at the Friars a few years ago. Standing by the front door you notice the arches of the old cloisters, the arches which were subsequently filled in by brick and stone so as to form passages along two sides of the house. But Colonel Shaw-Hellier followed up the foundations and discovered that the old cloisters formed a quadrangle and the present gravelled square in front of the house is its site. Above these cloisters were probably dormitories. Inside that part of the cloisters which is preserved the cells of the monks can be seen, each with a small window, but no fireplace. On one side of the square—a continuation of the present dining room—the chapel stood, extending beyond the walls of the quadrangle, and in one corner was found a vault containing bones. Directly opposite the front door and on the spot now covered by a lawn were discovered traces of the old chapter house.

There is not much of the interior to remind us of a priory beyond the enclosed cloisters and cells, for when Sir John Banks determined to transform it into a residence he went to work with a will and evidently with ungrudging hand. No less a person than Inigo Jones did he employ and the work of this famous decorator is to be seen in many parts of the house. The enclosed cloisters were paved with black and white marble, the staircase was crowned with some beautiful floral decoration, while in the large apartment known as the ball-room are gorgeous plaster festoons of fruit and flowers, exquisitely painted. The colour is slightly faded, but even now they appear so real that, brightened by gaslight, the grapes hang almost as luscious and the roses almost as natural as the fruit and flowers which they represent. In the drawing-room the colours have been painted over white but the freize of festoons looks wonderfully chaste.

The present ball room was the old refectory, but the dining-room is a modern building. A small stone spiral staircase can be seen at one corner of the old cloisters and an image stood here not long since. These stone steps are supposed to have led to the private rooms of the Prior, and this corner was the old entrance. Looking just outside you will see an archway which was filled in only a short time ago and this no doubt was the original entrance to the priory—when the site of the present front door was a part of the cloisters.

There is a story told about the little ante-room close by the drawing-room which is worth recording, although I fear that it cannot withstand the unrelenting blow of hard fact. It was said that Anne Boleyn from this apartment wrote to her ardent lover, Sir Richard Wyatt, at neighbouring Allington Castle, and actually described in a letter the beautiful festoons that adorned her room. But, unfortunately for the story, Inigo Jones, the great architect who designed the decorations, was not born in Anne Boleyn's time. Still there is but little doubt that Ann Boleyn was wont to stay at the Friars before she fell before the regal charms and splendour of Henry the Eighth, before she jilted the truest, noblest lover that ever maiden had—Sir Richard Wyatt.

What a strange fascination must Anne Boleyn have possessed—charms so wonderful that they hid entirely the defects which would make some women repulsive. One writer of her day says that on her left hand was the slight indication of a sixth finger, one of her teeth projected and on her throat was a wen which she always kept covered by a jewelled band. Yet so lovely was she to look upon that a French writer says you could not see her without loving her. Here is an early impression of Sir Thomas Wyatt: "At this time was presented to the eye of the English Court the rare and admirable beauty of the fresh and young lady, Anne Boleyn, whose beauty, passing sweet and cheerful, was enhanced by a nobility of manner, mildness and majesty more than words can express."

But to return to the Friars where Anne spent much of her time. If the interior has lost its cold monastic look under the warmth of modern comforts the same cannot be said of the old courtyard. A glance here and we seem to fall back into the days of long ago. It is a huge court, with a great number of buildings all around it, some now used as outhouses, some empty and out of repair, but none of them robbed of their original appearance. Gables and plaster walls, stone floors and brick, heavy unwieldy doors are all around us. The most interesting chamber is the old monks' kitchen, a huge place with many traces of its culinary utility still apparent. Just outside, let into the roof, is built a tiny dormer in which hung the bell that called the friars to duty or maybe rang the dinner hour to hungry pilgrims. The bell is gone but the old wheel and beam remain.

In one corner of the courtyard we find the original water entrance— the way through which visitors and monks came when they rowed to Aylesford by the Medway. And here, no doubt, the sporting old friars used to fish, for in those days the stream ran clear and merrily past the wall upon which you can well imagine the fishermen sat basking in the sun, dangling their plump legs, cracking jokes or muttering paternosters and pitting their own shrewd cunning against the cunning of the fish. And, bless you, I firmly believe they succeeded. For who could beat a holy friar at subterfuge, if all we hear be true? Can't you see him, a white-gowned, ghostly-looking fisherman, stealing down to the water's edge at dead of night and throwing ground bait in the pool. Then a sleepless anxious rest of a few hours upon his hard trestle. Up again at daybreak. Out through the creaking entrance gate once more. Hist! What is that? A splash, a rise. Yes, the roach, the fat roach are there, and the coarse bream and the piratical perch. Slowly creeps the fisherman, with body bent, so that the orange flash from rising sun shall throw no shadow over the water. With a twist of the wrist and the lightest touch he drops the baited hook. Away swims the float down stream. But only for a moment. The next instant it has gone. A strike, a tightened line, the run of a reel; then a plunge, a splash and within the meshes of a landing net struggles a two-pound roach upon the mossy steps. It is only one of many. The friar's cunning has encompassed the cunning of the fish.

Talking of fishing reminds me that a large pond is still to be seen near the house and it is supposed that the monks used to keep this as a reserve for fish.   Up at Tottington they owned the pools known at the present day as the Fishpond ; and probably the fish they caught there and in the Medway were placed in this old pond near the priory, ready for a rainy day.

Many years ago the people of neighbouring Burham revelled in the possession of a spring, whose waters were reverenced for the virtues they possessed.   Not only would they heal the sick but a sinner might come here and heal himself from sin—for a consideration.   Pilgrims came from all parts to test the power of the spring. But the Carmelites were too deep for the rustics of Burham. They obtained the consent of Richard the Second to run off the water to the Friars at Aylesford, an arrangement which brought it within their grasp and at the same time enabled them to take the tributes of pilgrims.   They not only obtained a fine supply of clear drinking water, but filled their coffers too.

Below in the cellars are supposed to be entrances of subterranean passages leading to Boxley Abbey and other places.   This tradition has given rise to a strange story.   Many an inquisitive being, so it is said, had entered one of these passages never to return.   They were lost, absolutely blotted out from sight, just as a stone disappears in a muddy pool.   At last came a pluckly old man, a fiddler, and he determined to fathom the mystery.   " When I enter," quoth he, " I will start to play my fiddle, and as I proceed through the darkness you will trace me by the sound."   And into the jaws of the unknown he strutted. The solemn cadences of a solemn march came from the opening and then for several minutes rose from below, penetrating the earth above, and heard by anxious hearers.   Then came a long, piteous, heart-thrilling note.   And after that ?   Silence !   Deathly silence.   No one followed the old fiddler. They shrank from the spot and it is said that the entrance was sealed up.   Rough on the plucky old fiddler, you will say.